PORTFOLIO

ECONOMICS WITHOUT TEARS

Ashok Sanjay Guha is Professor Emeritus at the School of International Studies at Jawaharlal Nehru University (JNU). Educated at Presidency College, Kolkata, and Harvard University, he returned to India as professor of economics at the School of International Studies. He has been associated with the university since its inception and still teaches there—a lifelong relationship only interrupted at times by visiting professorships at Yale, UCLA, UC Berkeley, Georgetown University, the universities of Colorado, Syracuse and Melbourne, and the Institute of Development Studies at Sussex. He has published in most of the world's leading economic journals. He has authored *An Evolutionary View of Economic Growth*, besides editing and contributing substantially to *Trade, Growth and Industrial Structure* and *Markets and Morals*. He also writes frequently in the popular press on a wide variety of subjects. He lives in Gurgaon with his wife and daughter.

ADVANCE PRAISE FOR THE BOOK

'In this concise book on economic theory for beginners, Ashok Guha focuses on some of the most important ideas in economics, which, because of their complexity, are usually treated in more advanced books, and brings out their core content with simple examples, telling anecdotes and easy-to-grasp analytical reasoning—all with a kind of lucidity that is exemplary. The topics chosen will grab the attention of all those who are curious about the discipline of economics but do not yet have a technical background. I wish a large readership for this short book'—Pranab Bardhan, Professor of the Graduate School, Department of Economics, University of California, Berkeley

'Ashok Guha is one of the most impressive Indian economists today. His book, *Economics without Tears*, demonstrates that he is also a gifted writer who can put across economics to a wider audience. This is a book that deserves to be read by the multitude who have become sceptical of the relevance of economics to policymaking to benefit mankind'— Jagdish Bhagwati, University Professor, Economics, Law and International Affairs, Columbia University

ECONOMICS WITHOUT TEARS

A NEW APPROACH TO
AN OLD DISCIPLINE

ASHOK SANJAY GUHA

PORTFOLIO
PENGUIN

PORTFOLIO

USA | Canada | UK | Ireland | Australia
New Zealand | India | South Africa | China

Portfolio is part of the Penguin Random House group of companies
whose addresses can be found at global.penguinrandomhouse.com

Published by Penguin Random House India Pvt. Ltd
7th Floor, Infinity Tower C, DLF Cyber City,
Gurgaon 122 002, Haryana, India

First published in Portfolio by Penguin Random House India 2016

ISBN 9780143426714

Typeset in Sabon by Manipal Digital Systems, Manipal
Printed at Thomson Press India Ltd, New Delhi

www.penguinbooksindia.com

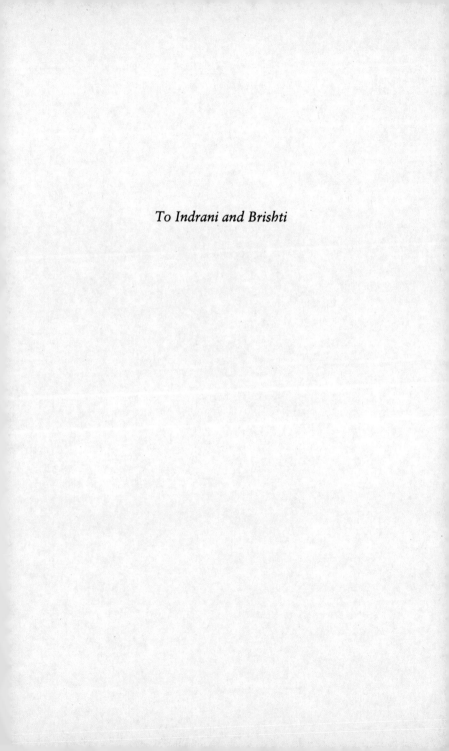

To Indrani and Brishti

Contents

Preface

Forty years ago, I was assigned the task of introducing economics to the students pursuing their master's in international relations at JNU. These students were some of the best and the brightest in the university, as their subsequent contributions towards the growth of the nation were to prove. However, they were primarily students of history, political science and sociology, with a sparse sprinkling of those pursuing literature and science. Hardly any had prior acquaintance with economics; and to a man (or woman), they were terrified of mathematics.

As someone trained in mainstream economics, with its mathematical rigour and uncompromising logical structure, I was thus confronted with two problems. First, how could I create and sustain in my students an enthusiasm for the subject I was supposed to teach? Could I somehow link it up with their primary interests, which were definitely not those of textbook economics? Second, how could I clarify the basic concepts of a discipline that had become increasingly mathematical without enmeshing them in mathematical methods and jargon that was sure to induce a state of uncomprehending somnolent boredom if not intellectual paralysis in my students?

This book provides an attempted solution, devised after many decades of interaction with students, to these twin problems.

In the process of working out my ideas, I made two important discoveries. First, while mathematics is a wonderful tool for explaining things to anyone whose mind works better with numbers and symbols than with words, it is by no means as indispensable to an understanding of economics as it is generally made out to be. Given an apt choice of words, the basic concepts of the discipline can be explained to the intelligent reader without any math whatsoever. This includes some, though not all, of the most advanced and contemporary ideas as well. Mathematics contributes chiefly in the generalization of results from two to many dimensions, but relatively few economic insights are gained in the process. Otherwise math adds more to esoteric quality than to intellectual clarity.

Second, economics is fun. It has serious implications, no doubt. But like all voyages of intellectual discovery, the process of learning economics is driven by a sense of wonder and amusement at the surprises, paradoxes and puzzles that confront us at every turn of the road and by the unsuspected answers that the journey provides to the questions that haunt us. If I succeed in communicating some of this to my readers, I will consider the writing of this book an enterprise that has been well worth its while.

PART I

Chapter 1

The Fundamental Problem of Economics

What is economics? Lionel Robbins, of the London School of Economics, famously defined the discipline as the study of the optimal use of scarce resources to satisfy unlimited wants.[1] The conventional textbook presents Robinson Crusoe on his lonely island, puzzling about how to use his limited resources and time to best satisfy his requirements, as the prototype of the applied economist. Robbins's definition and the Robinson Crusoe model are, in my opinion, misleading: they miss the essence of economics— the fact that it is a *social science*. They are more about the mathematics of maximization than about what goes on in any actual economy.

---

[1] Lionel Robbins, *An Essay on the Nature and Significance of Economic Science* (London: Macmillan, 1932).

Economics as a field of inquiry began with a very different question: a question that might be called the fundamental problem of economics.

As we all know, an economy is a system that involves millions of people—workers, producers, consumers, managers, financiers, brokers, students, teachers—all working to achieve their own separate goals in thousands of different environments—at home, in mills, in factories, in mines, on farms, in offices, in schools. It is a system of truly bewildering size and complexity. Consider what is involved when a certain Julie in Delhi buys a bar of chocolate. Her chocolate contains cocoa that comes from beans grown on a farm in Ghana and processed in Accra. It contains sugar produced from cane grown in Mauritius and milk drawn from cows in a dairy in Holland. The chocolate is made and packed in a Belgian factory and shipped out to Mumbai on a Greek ship, registered in Panama and manned by an Indian crew. In Mumbai, a Marathi dock worker transfers it to a truck driven by a Sikh all the way to the warehouse of a Marwari wholesaler in Sadar Bazar in Delhi. From there, a Haryanvi salesman carries it to a retailer, and it reaches the final consumer, Julie. Thousands of different people the world over have interacted in bringing Julie her bar of chocolate. And none of them know what she or anyone else in this network is doing, or even who they are.

Imagine a system with only a fraction of this complexity. Consider a situation where thousands of people are trying to drive to their own separate destinations without any traffic lights to guide them. As anyone can see, the outcome will be a nightmare—mile-long traffic jams at every intersection, turning all roads into a mass of immobile vehicles and angry drivers, honking, yelling, cursing, fighting, but going nowhere at all.

Why isn't the economy a similar chaotic mess? Why don't millions of people, completely disconnected from each other, and functioning in total anonymity, create an anarchy in which no one gets what they want? How, in fact, does the economy work as smoothly as it generally seems to? How does potential chaos turn into order? This is the fundamental problem of economics. Economics is basically about this miracle and it was about this that Adam Smith,[2] in 1776, wrote in *The Wealth of Nations*, generally regarded as the starting point of economics as a discipline.

The fundamental problem of economics then is that of *coordination*. Economists try to understand how billions of disparate and dispersed activities by millions of people knit together to produce order. How can this coordination be achieved?

COORDINATION BY COMMAND

One obvious way to achieve coordination is by the command of a central authority (which tells everyone precisely what to do on the basis of a well thought-out and coherent plan) and obedience on the part of everyone else. The centrally planned socialist economies were run according to such command and obedience principles. However, there are other, smaller command systems as well. Firms, armies, families, cricket teams, orchestras and film units are all command systems in which a central authority makes the decisions which everyone is supposed to implement thereafter.

---

[2] Adam Smith, *The Wealth of Nations* (1776).

How do command systems work? First, information is collected about all the individuals and all the areas covered by the system and transmitted to the central authority. Second, this information is processed by the authority and a decision is made about what each individual should precisely do, how and when. Third, these decisions are announced and enforced. Each of these stages has its own costs.

Consider just the informational costs, to begin with. The information requirement of a command system multiplies exponentially as its size increases. One needs, for example, information about all the possible relationships in the economy; and as the number of members in it increases, the number of possible relationships in it increases far more rapidly. As the number of individuals increases from two to three to four to five, the number of possible bilateral relationships alone increases from one to three to six to ten with a proportional growth in information requirement. And then there are trilateral, quadrilateral and other multilateral relationships. For the entire economy, the information requirement is truly vast and well beyond the capacity of even the most sophisticated supercomputer to store or process. The collection of so much information is immensely costly—it requires an army of agents, who have to be withdrawn from productive work.

Further, since these agents have their own objectives, not generally identical to the central authority's, they have every incentive to strategically distort their reports to the authority so as to derive personal benefit—the *principal–agent* problem. Income tax officers, for example, are required to accurately report a taxpayer's income to the government, but have a strong personal incentive to come to a private agreement to under-report it in exchange for a bribe. There is an often-told story of beautiful fake villages peopled by men posing as happy peasants, created on a riverbank by the minister Grigory Potemkin. He did this to impress Catherine the Great of Russia on her voyages of inspection to the Crimea. This may be apocryphal. But there is little doubt about the glowing reports of the success of the Great Leap Forward supplied to Mao Ze Dong during the greatest famine of the twentieth century by agents who feared the fate that awaits bearers of bad news. Principal–agent problems, of course, occur in many other contexts. In firms, for example, employers and employees share a principal–agent relationship. Shareholders, who are the real owners of the firm, would like to maximize its share value, but must operate through managers who are more interested in their salaries, bonuses and perks. Managers, in turn, function through their agents, the workers, whose natural inclination is to shirk as much as possible without being caught. None of these problems, however, match the scale and pervasiveness of the principal–agent problems that arise when a government seeks to plan and coordinate the activities of an entire economy.

Once the mass of information that this requires is assembled, there are costs involved in making decisions based on it. This is partly because processing this mass of information is expensive. Partly however, it is because of conflicts of opinion within the central authority about alternatives, except of course where the authority is a monolithic dictator, and the problem is of distilling these clashing opinions (or preferences) of individual members of the authority into a coherent collective decision. The authority may frame decision-making rules to resolve these conflicts: majority voting, for instance, or a two-third majority rule for important issues like constitution amendments, or unanimity in jury trials. However, one of the most famous results in modern economics—*Arrow's impossibility theorem*, which won the Nobel Prize for its creator, Kenneth Arrow[3]—shows that there cannot exist a non-dictatorial decision rule that yields rational collective decisions for every possible configuration of individual preferences. What does this mean? I shall illustrate by what is known as the *Paradox of Voting*. Discovered by the mathematician Marquis de Condorcet and elaborated, among others, by the Oxford mathematician Charles Lutwidge Dodgson (better known by his pseudonym Lewis Carroll), the Paradox of Voting visualizes three voters—A, B and C—choosing between three alternatives—X, Y and Z. Their preferences are distributed between the alternatives as follows:

1.   A prefers X to Y to Z.
2.   B prefers Y to Z to X.
3.   C prefers Z to X to Y.

Then, in a sequence of bilateral votes, X would win over Y, Y over Z and Z over X, so that no consistent and rational choice is possible.

Assuming that these problems have somehow been resolved, we are now faced with the costs of enforcement. The central authority has to ensure that its decisions are implemented, that people follow its commands. This implies that the authority must monitor the performance of every individual in the economy and design and enforce a set

---

[3] Kenneth J. Arrow, *Social Choice and Individual Values* (New York: Wiley, 1951).

of sanctions and rewards that would ensure compliance. We are now faced with a different, but equally massive, information problem requiring its own set of spies and informers also withdrawn from the productive activity and its agency costs (due to these spies falsifying their reports to the authority in order to serve their own personal interests). We have, in short, a police state, but not an efficient one, since who will police the police? It is important, however, to recognize that a secret police is an essential component in the design of a central planning system.

COORDINATION THROUGH THE MARKET: THE INVISIBLE HAND

The costs of running a large command system are then enormous. Is there a better mode of coordination? The first great discovery of economics is that there does exist such a coordination system. It is the free competitive market in which everyone reacts to a given set of prices. The price of a good tells you about its relative scarcity or abundance. If the price is high, you know that the good is scarce—you can make money by selling more of it, and you can save money by buying less. If you act according to your self-interest, selling more and buying less of the high-priced good, the scarcity of the good will be moderated. If the price is low, you are encouraged to do the opposite, thus eliminating any excess of the good in the market. The price is the *signal* that gives you the minimum information that induces you, in your own self-interest, to act in a way that restores order in the market, by coordinating the actions of sellers with those of buyers, all without anybody knowing anything more about the other participants in the market. The price system dispenses with the costs of collecting information since it does not need any. It eliminates the costs of collective decision-making since all decisions are made by individuals without any collective interference. And it does away with enforcement costs since it works entirely through the voluntary actions of individuals.

The role of the price as the signal of the relative abundance or scarcity of the good is effective as long as people react to it as a given parameter over which they have no influence—*the parametric function of prices*—as long as they are *price-takers*. If, however, they are big enough buyers or sellers of the good to be able to affect its price, the signalling value of price gets blurred. On the other hand, in a market so large that no individual can manipulate prices—a competitive market—coordination is achieved between millions of people all doing their own thing in complete ignorance of each other, without the intervention of a commanding authority, by the magic as it were of what Adam Smith called an *invisible hand*.

The miraculous role of the impersonal competitive price system as the creator of order amidst the potential chaos of an economy and its superiority to any man-made command system is the first major discovery of economics. However, the price system is not totally costless. Transactions in the market are attended by transaction costs, some, but not all, of which can be taken care of by the market itself. Transaction costs are of three kinds:

1. The costs of searching for the right partner or the right good to buy or to produce and sell (e.g. house or job hunting).
2. The costs of negotiating a deal (e.g. the costs of bargaining or of preparing and concluding an enforceable contract).

3. The costs of enforcing the contract (e.g. the costs of ensuring that my contractor doesn't abscond with my advance payment or the borrower with the loan that I have just given him).

While search and contracting costs can be minimized by hiring specialized intermediaries (brokers, lawyers, accountants) who get paid for, and therefore have an incentive to develop specialized knowledge and skill in their respective jobs, enforcement costs pose more of a problem. Enforcement requires the use or threat of coercion, either of direct force or indirectly through the penalties imposed by the courts and the law and order machinery. And since coercion is not part of the voluntary processes of the market, security of contract cannot be guaranteed within the framework of the market without the intervention of some coercive authority such as the police or the courts.

PROPERTY RIGHTS: PRIVATE AND PUBLIC GOODS

A market transaction consists of the exchange of property rights: I surrender to you my ownership rights over a particular object and you in return transfer to me the right to another object or a certain sum of money. I cannot sell you what I do not own. There may, of course, be people who are still prepared to buy it from me. In the Bollywood movie *Bunty aur Babli*, Rani Mukerji, claiming to be the Uttar Pradesh chief minister, sells the Taj Mahal to an American billionaire. But then, naïve American billionaires are exceptional. In general, only those goods can be traded in the market (and will therefore be produced for it) over which people can acquire property rights—only those goods which, in short, are *appropriable*.

But what is the right of property? Its essence does not lie in possession: a thief possessing stolen goods or a tenant occupying a rented house does not acquire property rights over what they possess or occupy. The right of property is the exclusive right to use or make decisions about the use of any object. Of course, there are limits to what I can do with my property. Suppose, for example, that I own a hammer. I can use it to drive nails into a piece of wood, but I cannot use it to hit you on the head. Subject to such limitations on what I can do with my hammer, only I, or those authorized by me, can use it. Exclusiveness—the ability to restrict the access of others to the object, to put up a sign saying 'No trespassing' and to back it up effectively—is the essence of property rights. Not all goods, however, permit exclusions. Given the current state of technology, it may be prohibitively costly to restrict the access of others to certain goods (air, for example, or roads for pedestrians or cyclists). These goods cannot then be sold in, or produced for, private markets.

We have, therefore, two classes of goods: *private goods*, which permit exclusions and are hence appropriable, and what might be called *public goods*, which are non-excludable, non-appropriable and can therefore only be produced if a coercive authority finances their production out of payments (taxes) that it extracts from the members of society. In some cases (air, for example), production is unnecessary—the public good is freely available; not so in others. Protection of contracts, of all property rights, or indeed of life itself is, for instance, a public good that requires an expensive judicial and police apparatus for its production. It is a public good because catching a thief benefits not only his immediate victim (through possible recovery of the stolen goods) but also everyone else who has one less criminal to contend with. It cannot, however, be supplied unless the government pays for it. There are many other examples of public goods.

Defence is a prime example of a good that would be drastically under-produced if left to the market. When I defend my territory against an invader, I willy-nilly defend yours as well. You, therefore, have a strong temptation to free-ride on my efforts. By a symmetrical argument, I have an equally strong inducement to free-ridership. With everyone free-riding, the invader can simply walk in and take possession of everyone's territory, assuming, of course, that he has condescended to spare everyone's life. To avoid this predicament, everyone may agree to put up a joint defence supported by a coercive authority that can compel contributions from everyone.

Law and order is an example that we have already touched upon. However, the apparatus of law and order embraces not just the executive arm of the police but also the codification of the law and the establishment of a judiciary and a judicial process, all of which have costs that no individual would voluntarily bear.

Civic hygiene, sanitation and public health are just as crucial, particularly to an urban economy. Though the inhabitants of the Indus Valley designed and created superb sewage systems well before 2000 BC and Roman cities developed basic sewerage as well, the rest of the world (and India after the collapse of the Harappan culture) had to await the Industrial Revolution before getting a sewer system. In Adam Smith's Edinburgh, the great centre of the Scottish Enlightenment, the city that was home not only to Smith, but to David Hume, Robert Burns, James Watt and Walter Scott as well, in the late eighteenth century, on the very eve of the Industrial Revolution, every evening was redolent with what were called 'the flowers of Edinburgh'—the contents of chamber pots emptied from upper-storey windows on to the heads of unwary pedestrians in the street below. The consequences, of course, were not merely unaesthetic, but lethal—the proliferation of diseases like cholera, typhus, typhoid and many others, and a consequent upsurge in death rates. But the advent of sanitation would have been impossible without an urban government that could tax the citizenry to finance it.

Public health measures fall in the same category. Inoculation, vaccination, etc. are public goods because anyone who receives vaccination confers on others an unintended benefit—he ensures that fewer germs are around to infect others, just as thieves in prison mean fewer thieves for the population at large to contend with. And these, of course, are benefits from which it is impossible to exclude unintended beneficiaries.

More generally, the protection of the environment cannot be left to private decision-makers, because everyone has an incentive to free-ride on the efforts of others and none to bear a cost himself. Indeed, environmental problems have increasingly acquired a global dimension with poisoning of the atmosphere resulting in global warming and of the oceans resulting in species loss. We are now confronted not just with the incentive to free-ride on the citizens of a particular state but with the determination of every nation-state to free-ride on the efforts of the rest of the world.

Roads are yet another set of goods to which it is exceedingly expensive to deny access to anyone. Not motorized highways of course, where there are toll gates at which potential free-riders can be intercepted. But traditional roads cannot possibly be policed along their entire length. So free-riders cannot be excluded, private citizens have no incentive to build such roads and their construction becomes one of the inescapable duties of the state. All the great empire builders of history have also been great road builders: the Incas, the Romans, Napoleon, Ashoka, Ghiyasuddin Balban, Sher Shah Suri and Akbar, amongst others.

A public good of great historical importance is large-scale irrigation and flood control. In semi-arid regions or regions of uncertain rainfall located in the valleys of great rivers, life often depends on the irrigation systems based on these rivers. Further, since the rivers are typically prone to devastating floods, survival requires flood control. The beneficiaries of these services, however, will not voluntarily pay for them. Each farmer in the floodplain knows that his access to flood control is independent of whether he personally pays for it or not—if he doesn't and the others do, he cannot be denied flood control; if he does and others don't, he will not get it despite his contribution. It may not be too easy to exclude him from irrigation benefits either; it may be relatively simple to divert water from adjacent irrigation canals without paying for it or tapping subsoil water from a water table that has risen because of irrigation nearby. But if the potential beneficiaries will not voluntarily pay for the waterworks, a coercive authority is needed for their creation. And indeed such river valleys have been the cradles of powerful states whose prime function seems to have been flood control and irrigation—Pharaonic Egypt astride the Nile, the ancient Mesopotamian empires on the Tigris–Euphrates, the Chinese dynasties that ruled the Hwang Ho basin, even perhaps the Mughal empire based on its heartland in the Ganga–Jumna basin. The German historian Karl Wittfogel developed a theory of hydraulic despotism, linking state power with the provision of large-scale irrigation and flood control.[4]

Other examples of public goods are traffic control, the missing link in the story of traffic chaos with which we began this chapter, and lighthouses. In all such cases, the beneficiaries have no incentive to pay, since free-riding is easy.

Thus, the market cannot survive, nor can the society, without an infrastructure of indispensable public goods, provided by a coercive authority like the state, and funded by compulsory payments like taxes. These constitute *the economic basis of the state.*

It is crucial, however, to distinguish between public goods in the sense that economists use the term—goods that private enterprise cannot produce—from goods that it can but that the state is currently producing for whatever reason. The latter are private goods produced by the state in possible competition with private individuals. This includes not just the supposed classic examples of government overreach—bakeries and hotels in the public sector—but also mines, heavy industries, electricity generation and public transport operated by public enterprise and banks, schools and hospitals run by the government. The state injects itself into these fields not because private enterprise cannot, but because of a variety of other reasons. It may wish to subsidize these goods and services from the general budget so as to improve income distribution, a somewhat inadequate reason since it could always subsidize their production by private individuals at low prices. Alternatively, it may be that, as Pandit Nehru

---

[4] Karl Wittfogel, *Oriental Despotism: A Comparative Study of Total Power* (New Haven: Yale University Press, 1957).

often said, 'the state should control the commanding heights of the economy.' Private goods produced by the government do not establish the indispensability of the state. Public goods (in our sense of the term) do.

In exceptional cases, societies have invented their own methods of sustaining economic transactions without the coercive apparatus of the state. These examples of what is called *spontaneous order* are briefly touched upon in the following box.

SPONTANEOUS ORDER

Nature offers many examples of self-organizing systems: the growth of babies in the womb, the formation of crystals and snowflakes, the birth of life through the emergence of the self-replicating DNA molecule, the growth of languages and the evolution of the universe itself. Economics, too, displays occasional instances of a similar kind. While markets generally require external supports like the machinery of law and order, they may sometimes evolve a spontaneous order without external legal support. I cite two examples from history.

The Maghrebi Trader's Coalition[5]

A group of Jewish merchants, based in north-west Africa, traded all over the Mediterranean from the eleventh to

[5] For a detailed analysis, see Avner Greif, 'Contract Enforceability and Economic Institutions in Early Trade: The Maghribi Traders' Coalition', *The American Economic Review* 83 (1993): 525–48.

the thirteenth century. They had no legal protection in the Christian and Muslim countries where they traded, yet were conspicuously successful over a vast span of space and time. How and why? In particular, each merchant needed a local agent in each location where he traded. How did the principal ensure that the agent did not cheat him? Essentially, the community developed three conventions. First, all agents were hired from within the community. Second, any Maghrebi accused of cheating by any other was immediately boycotted by the entire community—a multilateral punishment strategy (MPS). Third, any Maghrebi who did not participate in this boycott was boycotted by the rest of the community.

Since no coercive apparatus existed, the system had to be self-enforcing. How did MPS ensure this? Basically, an agent may cheat if his expected lifetime return from cheating today (followed by dismissal) exceeded that from a lifetime of honesty. There exists a minimum wage that is high enough to deter cheating. How high this wage has to be depends on the payoff that the agent expects after cheating. This is a function primarily of the probability of re-employment. MPS reduces this probability to zero, so that a relatively low wage may guarantee honesty. If, on the other hand, the punishment is not collective but individual—a bilateral punishment strategy (BPS)—the agent stands a better chance of being rehired after cheating and dismissal. It would then be difficult to deter him from cheating unless a much higher wage is paid.

The Fundamental Problem of Economics 19

Now consider a merchant who must choose between hiring an agent who is believed never to have cheated and another who is believed to have done so. The latter has already lost his reputation for honesty. All he stands to lose in future if he cheats the merchant who is foolish enough to hire him is the prospect of being re-employed by this particular merchant. Therefore, a much higher wage is required to persuade him to be honest than for the agent with a reputation for honesty. It is, therefore, more profitable for the merchant to hire the agent who has never cheated.

Similarly, if the merchant were to hire an agent outside his community, the latter's prospects of future employment would be essentially unaffected if he cheats the merchant. Since the agent's community doesn't punish him for cheating an outsider, he would be facing only a BPS—the merchant must pay him a high wage to keep him honest and this would be less profitable than hiring a supposedly honest agent from within the community.

Thus, the Maghrebi adherence to the three conventions and the consequent imperative to be honest did not have to be forced on them by an authority. Each individual had a personal interest in following the rules as long as the others did so. Similar self-sustaining reputation mechanisms have evolved in most small communities that have functioned for long periods of time in alien environments—the Cantonese merchants in South East Asia, the Marwaris, Gujaratis, Parsees and Chettiyars in India, the Ismailis in the Muslim

world, the Huguenots in France, and the Hasidic Jews
who controlled the diamond trade from Antwerp and
New York. Among Marwari and Gujarati traders, for
example, oral contracts are common, and in order to
do business, it is essential that one should protect one's
imaan or reputation for keeping one's word. *Be-imaani*
or breach of promise is the most serious accusation one
can level against a merchant, because all other merchants
will shun the *be-imaan*, the one who has broken his
word.

The Champagne Fairs

A key issue in a reputation mechanism like that used by
the Maghrebi merchants is dissemination of information.
How is the news that an individual has cheated to
reach all those who are to punish him multilaterally?
At the time of occurrence, this is private information
known only to one principal and his agent. How does
it become common knowledge? If the circulation of this
information is costly to the cheated individual, it will
not be worth his while to circulate it since, by doing
so, he will merely enable others to punish the cheat
but will not profit himself in any way. But then MPS
will unravel. The Maghrebis relied for their news on
continuous gossipy correspondence about themselves
and all others in their community. But this will not work
in a large group of anonymous people.

  The Champagne Fairs that were the focus of
international trade in medieval Europe represented

an assembly of such a large anonymous group. The fairs attracted participants from all over Europe, mostly beyond the jurisdiction and out of reach of the local Champagne authorities. One would have expected, therefore, that they would become hotbeds of cheating, losing credibility and soon dissolving in chaos. In fact, however, they continued successfully for centuries. The secret of their longevity probably lay in a mechanism more complex than the Maghrebi but based, like it, on MPS.[6]

The access to the fairs was controlled by the local authorities, the counts of Champagne. A merchant who had been cheated at the fair could complain to these authorities who, after investigating, could bar the wrongdoer from future fairs. There was, of course, the chance that the authorities might, for a consideration, collude with the cheats and allow them entry. However, this was minimized by the possibility that the wronged merchant might see the cheat at a future fair and initiate, not just individual, but collective punishment measures against the fair authorities. Almost all traders belonged to large associations known as guilds. A complaint by one of its members against Champagne for colluding in cheating would very likely induce the guild to advise all its members to switch their business from Champagne to a competing fair.

---

[6] For a complete analysis, see Brishti Guha, 'Who Will Monitor the Monitors? Informal Law Enforcement and Collusion at Champagne', *Journal of Economic Behavior and Organization* 83 (2012): 261–77.

Now the attraction of any trade fair depends largely on the number of participants. That is what determines the number of contacts one makes and contracts one signs at a fair. The defection of a large guild not only impairs the reputation of a fair for integrity, it also sharply reduces its attraction for merchants and induces other withdrawals in a cumulative downward spiral. Punishment is multilateralized with a vengeance. Such a threat is enough to deter most fair authorities from collusive cheating, even though there can be no recourse to a judicial process. In Champagne, it was enough to sustain the fairs for hundreds of years without any major damage to their credibility.

There are certain goods that are non-excludable but benefit only a subset of the individuals in society, e.g. the wage increases negotiated by a trade union or the price increases enforced by a cartel. These benefit the members regardless of whether they have individually borne the costs needed to achieve these increases. Therefore, trade unions and cartels, like the individuals in the examples of public goods cited above, face a free-rider problem: each member has no incentive to bear the sacrifices called for by collective action to increase wages or prices. If he shares the costs, but the other members don't, wages/prices will not rise; if he doesn't pay but all the others do, wages/prices will increase despite his free ride. In consequence, no one is willing to sacrifice, and collective action cannot be undertaken by the group unless the union or the cartel has some means of disciplining errant members. Unions, for example, ostracize blacklegs (members who do not join a strike) or, if they do not believe in such subtlety, simply have them beaten up by goons.

There are also public goods that are not producible, but exhaustible (*natural resource goods*)—fish in open waters, for example. These are public in the sense that no one can be denied access to them. So over-exploitation is inevitable (why?), leading to depletion and possible extinction of the resource ('*the tragedy of the commons*'). Nation states try to guard against this by asserting their ownership rights over their coastal waters and their contents, including fish. Unfortunately, the fish do not know this and migrate freely across territorial limits. This has led to episodes like the possibly apocryphal tale of the Japanese trawlers in the Bay of Bengal. The Japanese, according to this story, developed, among their many technological innovations, a kind of underwater music that fish found irresistible. Their trawlers therefore stood at anchor just outside India's territorial waters and played this submarine melody that seduced all the Indian fish into the waiting arms, or nets, of Japanese fishermen.

An error, often encountered in introductory economics textbooks, is to describe public goods as those that are *non-rivalrous goods* such that the amount consumable by one person is not diminished by the consumption of another. Viewership of a movie is a typical example. Such goods are better described as *club goods*—consumption by one club member does not affect what is consumable by another. However, entry to the club can certainly be restricted to those who would pay for it. There is no reason why such goods cannot be privately produced or sold, as Hollywood, Bollywood, Kollywood, Tollywood, etc. indicate.

COASE'S THEOREM

In all cases of public goods, there are discrepancies between the costs/benefits of using a good as perceived by the individual user and by society at large, between *private* and *social* costs/benefits, or between effects that are *internal* to the user and *externalities*—for example, between the personal benefits I derive from being vaccinated and the benefit this confers on others of reduced exposure to infection. The market, driven as it is by isolated private decisions, takes care only of private costs and internal effects, resulting in the neglect of externalities and non-production of public goods. But the production of public goods, funded by the government, is subject to all the costs and inefficiencies of the command system discussed earlier. Is there a solution to this dilemma?

A path-breaking result in modern economics asserts that there is. The Chicago economist Ronald Coase[7] developed this in his youth. Ignored at first, its importance seemed to increase with every passing decade and eventually won him the Nobel Prize at the age of ninety. Luckily, he was still alive, since there are no posthumous Nobel prizes.

Coase's theorem states that, whenever an externality exists, the market generates an incentive for a transfer of properties that would internalize the externality. To understand the meaning of this, consider the flood-control example. All farmers in the floodplain of a river would benefit from a dam that would protect their lands and increase their collective value by more than the cost of the dam. But given

---

7 Ronald Coase, 'The Problem of Social Cost', *Journal of Law and Economics* 3 (1960): 1–44.

the existing ownership pattern, the dam would never be built unless the farmers are coerced to pay for it. The market, however, generates incentives for a redistribution of land that could resolve this problem. It creates an opportunity for an entrepreneur to buy up all the flood-prone land, build the dam and then resell. If the increase in the value of the land exceeds the cost of the dam, it will be possible for the entrepreneur to pay the farmers more than the value of their flood-prone lands and yet make a profit on the transaction. The transfer of properties from the farmers to the entrepreneur enables him to capture the full benefits of the investment in flood control, to internalize what was an externality. What was a public good becomes a private good.

Coase's theorem however has a qualification. It works only if the transaction cost of the transfer of properties is small. In the present case, the transaction cost for the entrepreneur to buy from thousands of farmers may be substantial, particularly because after he has bought up most of the land, the remaining farmers may realize that their land is far more valuable to him than to them and hold out for an exorbitant price. Land acquisition for any large-scale enterprise, for road-building or other infrastructural development, is beset by a similar hold-up problem. Thus, Coase's theorem does not eliminate all public goods, or even most of the important ones.

It applies, however, in a wide range of cases. Examples:

1. A confectioner sets up a shop next to a dentist. The noise of the confectioner's grinding machinery penetrates the dentist's chamber and waiting room, leaving his patients in agony. Imagine you are in a dentist's chamber, already clutching your face in pain, and then you hear this

grinding machinery. It would simply drive you crazy. The dentist's practice suffers in consequence. What can he do to improve things? Coase's theorem suggests that he could buy off the confectioner, bribing him to move elsewhere if the costs of doing so are less than the loss he suffers in consequence of the confectioner's proximity. If not, hard luck for the dentist and his patients—their sufferings are less than the benefits the confectioner derives from his present location.

2. I like to write my papers at night. Unfortunately, that is precisely the time my neighbour, who is just learning to play the violin, selects for his daily practice. The resulting cacophony reduces my output of papers to zero. It also turns me to a crazy insomniac. Since I am an economist, I invoke Coase's theorem. Coase advises me to consider buying up the apartment next door and letting it out only on the strict condition that the tenant should not play the violin at night. If I do not feel this to be worthwhile, I will have no option but to grin and bear it. I have, after all, chosen to endure an 'ordeal by fiddle' rather than to part with my money.

Both these examples involve one-on-one transactions, as opposed to many-on-one with flood control, so they involve lower costs and Coase's theorem works.

SUMMARY

I have argued that economics is fundamentally about the problem of coordination of the infinitely varied activities of vast numbers of individuals, each with his own private goals, so as to achieve order out of potential chaos. There are two ways by which coordination can be effected, by commands from and obedience to a central authority (as in central planning), or by an impersonal price-guided market.

At the heart of the coordination problem lies issues of information. Relative to central planning, the price system has the advantage of informational economy. It minimizes information requirements by decentralizing decision-making, thus reducing the need for agents with their own separate agendas.

However, the market has its own costs. The most indispensable of these are the enforcement of contracts and of property rights, both of which the market cannot ensure without the coercive authority of the state to back it up. More generally, the market can only supply private goods, goods that can be turned into private property by excluding 'outsiders'. However, for a large number of goods, some of them absolutely essential for survival, such exclusion is technologically impossible. These are public goods that must be supplied by a coercive authority, which can force the beneficiaries of these goods to contribute to their production and upkeep. Public goods, however, come with all the inefficiencies of the command system.

This dilemma was partially resolved by Ronald Coase. He argued that whenever a public good is potentially worthwhile under a given distribution of property, the market creates an incentive for a transfer of property that could turn the public good into a private one. If these transactions are costless, they would eliminate the public-good problem. However, transaction costs are often high, especially when large numbers of people are involved in the transaction and the possibility of a hold-up is real. So public goods, despite their inefficiency, remain an inescapable fact of economic life.

PROBLEMS

The reader is strongly advised to glance through the
following problems—as indeed through all problems in this
book—to clarify his understanding of the concepts outlined
as well as for fun.

1. The residents of Pun Pun Hostel at Pannalal Kachroo
    University (PKU) have a problem. In the best egalitarian
    tradition of PKU, they share the mess bill equally among
    themselves. However, each resident finds himself much
    fatter than he would like to be, and also much poorer.
    Can you explain their predicament? What about a
    solution? Can a similar solution be employed to defray
    the costs of open-air movie shows at PKU?
2. Classify as private or public goods:
    a) A play performed in an auditorium.
    b) A radio broadcast of a play.
    c) Steel produced by a public corporation.
    d) A painting displayed in a gallery of fine arts.
    e) A mural that adorns the front of a building.
3. Edible sea fish constitute one of the world's most readily
    exhaustible and endangered resources. Why?
4. International commodity agreements between major
    producers of primary exports (wheat, coffee, copper, tin
    and, of course, oil) in order to restrict output and raise
    prices have been fairly common. None of these have,
    however, been successful for any length of time. Explain.

Chapter 2

Information and the Economic Problem

Information (and misinformation) is central to the functioning of the economy. I argued in the last chapter that the free market has the enormous advantage of lower information requirements than alternative systems of economic organization. It does not, however, dispense with all requirements for information beyond what is conveyed by the ruling market prices. Much of this information is known to one side of the market but not to the other—known to the buyer perhaps but not to the seller or vice versa. The possessor of information can often exploit this *information asymmetry* to his advantage. He cannot readily dispel it by credibly conveying the facts to the other party when that is to his advantage.

The crucial importance of information is well illustrated by the often-told story of the Rothschild fortune—one that has been disputed by many. But whether true or false, it remains one of the best examples of the economic value of information. The story goes that the vast Rothschild fortune was the result of the events of 18–21 June 1815, the Battle of Waterloo and its immediate aftermath. The head of the Rothschild family then was Nathan Rothschild, a businessman known less for fabulous wealth than for the fact that he always seemed to have his finger on the pulse of current events. The Battle of Waterloo was fought between the French under Napoleon Bonaparte and the British under the Duke of Wellington and their Prussian allies under Marshal Blucher, and it shaped the future of Europe. The early exchanges of the battle were rather inconclusive, but late in the afternoon, Napoleon launched his famous Imperial Guard and they drove the British back with fearful losses. Cartloads of British dead and wounded began streaming back to their base camp in Brussels, triggering a panic evacuation of the city, graphically described by William Thackeray in his novel *Vanity Fair*.

Knowing the importance of the battle, Rothschild had posted his spies on the highest hill overlooking Waterloo. They saw the French assault and the convoys of British casualties. But through their powerful field glasses, they also saw in the distance the columns of Prussian troops advancing to reinforce the British. They knew that Napoleon had shot his bolt and had no possible response left to the allied counter-offensive. The news of the impending allied victory was immediately dispatched to London. Rothschild had arranged for relays of fresh horses all the way to the ferry at Ostend and across the Channel from Dover to London, so that by the afternoon of 20 June, he knew of Napoleon's defeat. Meanwhile, by nightfall of 18 June, the French had been routed and a triumphant Wellington asked his aide-de-camp (ADC) to convey the good tidings to Downing Street. The ADC stopped at every bar on the way to celebrate, so that it was only by the evening of 21 June that the government learnt of the famous victory.

On the morning of that day, however, suspense still prevailed when Rothschild entered the stock exchange and stood by his favourite pillar in an attitude of deepest dejection. Given the absence of official news and Rothschild's reputation for omniscience, all eyes were focused on him. He waited until his body language had been noted by all observers; then, in a loud voice, he instructed his brokers to sell everything they had. Panic immediately ensued as every onlooker sought to imitate the supposed example of Rothschild. He had, however, instructed his men to wait until stocks touched rock-bottom and then to begin buying in small lots that could not immediately be traced back to him. By the evening, when the official news of Wellington's victory trickled in and the market rallied, Rothschild owned the city of London.

This is a classic example of the exploitation of informational asymmetry—indeed of its deliberate intensification—for personal advantage. Somewhat similar is the practice of insider trading which is considered illegal in most countries. However, the incidence and implications of asymmetric information for the economy are far more wide-ranging and far-flung than this, and it is to a consideration of these implications that we now turn.

THE LEMONS PROBLEM

The Rothschild story shows how a very temporary informational asymmetry may translate into huge profits for the holder of this temporary monopoly of knowledge. A less transient informational asymmetry that deeply affects how buyers and sellers make their decisions relates to the *quality* of the products being traded. The price system cannot credibly signal quality, leading to what is known as the *lemons problem*.[8] Consider the market for second-hand cars (lemons), where the buyer knows less about the quality of the cars than the seller. This informational asymmetry cannot be corrected. The buyer will not believe the seller's proclamations about quality. Nor can he assess the quality of a used car merely by inspection. The buyer therefore bases his offer for a particular used car on the average expected quality of cars of that make and vintage. The seller then has no incentive from the point of view of resale to maintain the quality of his car. Quality is costly, but he earns no quality premium in terms of resale value. He is induced therefore to run down his car, a temptation that economists describe as *moral hazard*. If he belongs to the few who insist on maintaining quality, he will be unable to resell his car as cheaply as the others and will therefore be driven out of the market by them—a phenomenon that economists call *adverse selection*. Both moral hazard and adverse selection reduce the average expected quality of cars on offer, so that buyers are willing to pay progressively less. Sellers' incentives to run

---

[8] George A. Akerlof, 'The Market for "Lemons": Quality Uncertainty and the Market Mechanism', *Quarterly Journal of Economics* 84 (1970): 488–500.

down their cars are thereby further reinforced, and more of the better cars are driven out of the market. Ultimately, only those cars are offered that no one is prepared to buy at any price and the used-car market collapses, a consequence that adversely affects all potential buyers and sellers of used cars.

The lemons problem is particularly acute when the buyers' and sellers' paths are unlikely to cross in future and when the one who faces moral hazard is anonymous (i.e. has no reputation to sustain). When you are buying from a wandering tradesman at a country fair, he is deterred from cheating you only by his (possibly elastic) conscience and a consideration of whether he can abscond with the proceeds before you discover what is wrong with your purchase. If, however, there are repeat encounters and if the seller has to protect a reputation that could be damaged by the reports of dissatisfied customers, the seller would indeed have an incentive to maintain quality.

So, in all such markets, either (1) long-term seller–buyer relationships develop as a guarantee of quality, or (2) intermediaries (used-car dealers, brokers, underwriters, auditors, etc.) emerge with a reputation to protect.

In thin markets, in less-developed regions, long-term patron–client relationships are typical. A strong bond of mutual loyalty develops between the customer and his butcher, fishmonger, grocer, baker, barber, doctor, banker or lawyer that overrides moral hazard and makes life easier.

In thicker, but more anonymous markets, intermediaries proliferate. Small manufacturers, based in less-developed countries, often need well-known multinational distributors to penetrate rich markets in the advanced world. Korea, still underdeveloped in the sixties and seventies, famously used Sears Roebuck to capture the multibillion dollar US ready-made men's garment market. Firms that seek capital through share issues or loans need auditors to attest to the soundness of their financial position and to certify that they have no history of decamping with the investor's money. The auditors need to be far fewer than the firms they audit, so that they can acquire a reputation for honesty—of not colluding with their clients to cover up malfeasance—so as to reassure investors about the safety of their investments.

The lemons problem reduces the efficiency of the price system. Patron–client relationships create little islands in which prices are settled by mutual bargaining; they are no longer parameters to which buyers and sellers must adjust. Intermediaries are individuals who are withdrawn from productive work simply to resolve the lemons problem and so represent some of its real costs.

It is important to recognize that asymmetric information is not a problem peculiar to the market-price system. Private information will not be automatically disclosed to the central planner as soon as planning replaces the market, and, if it is volunteered, its credibility will remain highly suspect. The possessor of private information is bound to exploit it for personal benefit with all the consequences we have dwelt on above.

The lemons problem pervades all economics. Its implications and consequences have shaped our economic institutions throughout history and continue to do so today, especially in the less-developed countries.

THE LEMONS PROBLEM IN THE CREDIT MARKET

Possibly the most important implications of the lemons problem relate to the credit market. Here, the lender doesn't know which borrower will have the intention or the capacity to repay and so indiscriminately charges everyone a high interest rate to cover the risk of default. This, in turn, increases the temptation to default. It also drives away honest borrowers who cannot afford the high interest rates, leading to escalation in the risk of default and consequently in the interest rate until only those borrowers remain who don't care how high the interest rate is since they don't intend to repay any way and the credit market collapses. How might lenders avert such a sequence of events?

First, they could ration credit on the basis of the collateral that the borrower offers as security for the loan. Loans are offered only to the wealthy; those without assets are denied access to the credit market. In the best biblical tradition, 'Him that hath, to him it shall be given, and from him that hath not shall be taken away even that which he hath.' With no prospect of consumption loans in the event of the failure of a risky enterprise, the poor must be averse to risk to survive. They cannot be innovative since any experiment with a new technology is necessarily high-risk. In consequence, they lag far behind the rich in the productivity race. The denial of production loans has much the same outcome. Producers need loans to supplement their personal resources whenever they embark on a large-scale enterprise or one that will bear fruit only in the long run. Most high-productivity projects have one or both of these characteristics. Denial of loans to the poor bars their entry into the world of high productivity. The rich are not similarly constrained. The large personal stake they can hold in any enterprise reassures lenders and shareholders-to-be and attracts loans and share capital. Thus, the concentration of wealth is cumulatively intensified. The lemons problem in the credit market is the single largest source of economic inequality.

Apart from its impact on the distribution of wealth and income, the denial of credit to the poor also shapes the nature of contracts and class relations. By forcing risk aversion on the poor, it drives them into contracts that minimize risk, contracts that offer them a fixed wage or a fixed crop share, thus wholly or partially insuring them against the income fluctuations that are an inescapable part of business, whether in agriculture, industry or services. Their rich partners in these contracts assume all or part of the risk of loss, but they also reap any windfall gains that may accrue. The rich profit earner is the *residual claimant* in the firm. He captures whatever remains after contractual payments have been made. If Sony loses money, it still has to pay its bankers the interest it promised and its workers their contractual wages, but if it enjoys a sudden business bonanza, it does not have to share it with anyone else; the owners (the shareholders) take it all in the form of higher dividends and share values.

But this arrangement determines more than the distribution of income. It also necessitates a particular structure of authority. Since the residual claimant is the only direct beneficiary of any wise decisions made by the firm, efficiency requires that he should be the decision-maker himself. That alone would ensure that the incentive for good decision-making is maximized. If it is not, the firm will be ousted by the competition of firms where decision-making is more efficient. Of course, the decision-maker must ensure that his decisions are implemented: he must be an enforcer with disciplinary powers. All this implies hierarchy with the residual claimant on top, so that the structure of the firm is dictated by the lemons problem.

A second way in which a lender may function in a climate of severe moral hazard would be to restrict his lending within the extended family circle. If he did so, he could mobilize the powerful force of family disapproval to discourage potential default. Also, since within the family, there are no secrets, the credit history of each borrower would be common knowledge. And of course, it would be easier to monitor the end use of any loan to ensure that it is not dissipated in an obviously unproductive way that adds nothing to the borrower's capacity to repay. The viability of credit transactions within, but not outside, the family accounts for the large role that family conglomerates have played in Asian economic development—from the zaibatsu and keiretsu of Japan and the Korean chaebol to the family business houses of the Chinese diaspora and those that have dominated the Indian economy for more than a century.

A third solution would be the interlinkage of credit with the labour, land or product markets; if I only lend to those who are dependent on me in another market—my employee, my tenant, the farmer whose produce I market—I have a powerful lever with which to compel repayment. I can deduct his wages, increase his rent or reduce the price I pay him if he delays the loan repayment.

Yet another method of lending to borrowers who have no security to offer involves collective responsibility for repayment. One lends, not to individuals but to small groups that assume collective liability. The borrower decides whom he wishes to form a group with. His interest is best served by forming a group with people whose attitudes to, and abilities for, repayment match his own. Each loan is small, so that the group has little incentive to decamp with it. Renewal of the loan is contingent on repayment. In consequence, every member of the group has a stake in repayment. He, therefore, monitors the use to which the loan has been put by the member primarily interested in it and presses the latter never to default. The lender taps into the pool of local knowledge about people through the process of group formation and ensures peer-group monitoring of and social pressure on the primary borrower for the sake of repayment. The Grameen Bank of Bangladesh is of course the best-known example of such a lending institution and it has had some success in making unsecured loans available to the poor.

LEMONS AND INSURANCE

In the insurance market, the insurer doesn't know if the insured will take due precautions to minimize the risk insured against. I may take out fire insurance and proceed immediately to set my house on fire. More generally, insurance creates a temptation for contributory negligence— the insuree tends to neglect costly precautions. Further, the insurer does not know in advance the insuree's attitude to risk, whether the latter is inclined to play safe or to gamble. He, therefore, charges everyone a high-enough premium to cover the cost of negligence by the insuree, thereby intensifying the moral hazard of the latter and discouraging the safer insurees from buying insurance altogether. Insurers are left only with high-risk insurees, consequently escalating premiums and the possible breakdown of the insurance market.

There are, of course, costly remedies. Insurance policies could provide for a minimum *deductible,* which would have to be paid by the insuree if the event insured against actually happens and which would therefore strengthen his incentive to take precautions, but it would increase the cost of insurance and shrink the insurance market. Alternatively, the insurance company may offer a menu of contracts: a high-premium, high-risk contract that gamblers may prefer as well as a low-premium, low-risk policy that safer insurees may like. Having thus separated his customers into identifiable groups, the insurer may impose a deductible on the gamblers but not the others. This may even eliminate the gamblers altogether and restrict his clientele to safe insurees alone, but only at the cost that higher risks will not be insured against and therefore may not be undertaken.

Alternatively, the extended family may itself provide insurance, just as it often provides credit. Protection against moral hazard would then have to depend on the bonds of kinship and the insider information about family members and their activities that flows along the family grapevine.

TECHNOLOGY LEMONS

In the technology market, the buyer cannot possibly know in advance the quality of the technology he is buying. He would need to know the minutiae of the technology in order to assess its quality, and if he did, he would hardly have needed to buy it. The buyer's ignorance tempts the seller to transfer inferior technologies. The buyer, knowing this, offers a low price, which, in turn, intensifies moral hazard and drives away the sellers of superior technology, so that the technology market may fold up. In each case, there is a risk of market failure and a cost to averting it. The consequence: technology transfer by foreign direct investment, rather than by technology lease and licensing. The foreign owner of a superior technology sets up a branch or subsidiary in the low-tech economy instead of selling or leasing his technology to a local firm.

LEMONS IN THE LABOUR MARKET

Hiring Lemons

In the job market, the employer doesn't know the ability of his new recruit—if he indiscriminately offers a wage geared to the average expected level of productivity, he will attract workers of lesser ability while driving away the more capable. This reduces the average productivity of his employees, inducing lower wage offers, further decline in productivity and so on in the usual vicious circle.

How could employers and employees protect themselves from a predicament so unpleasant to both? The employer could perhaps design an aptitude test to *screen* job applicants. The employee could *signal* his ability through some proxy (such as educational attainment).[9] Each of these devices has its own costs however. Employers who screen job applicants have to not only bear these costs but also face the possibility of competing employers free-riding on the information they have unearthed and bidding away their best discoveries at no cost to themselves. Signalling makes more sense despite its costs since the more capable worker would like some means of convincing potential employers about his ability. The low-ability worker has an equal interest in suppressing

---

[9] Michael Spence, 'Job Market Signaling', *Quarterly Journal of Economics*, 87 (1973): 355–74.

this information. However, as long as the advantage secured by high-quality individuals through the conveyance of information exceeds the costs they incur in the process, they will have an interest in it. What is this advantage? It is the difference between the terms they can get by establishing their quality and the terms that are offered to individuals of average quality. If there exists a hierarchy of qualities, then, once the best individuals have separated themselves from the general pool by establishing their quality, the second-best individuals have a similar incentive to separate themselves from the average of those who remain. And so on, until the cost of conveying information matches the advantage in terms that the last group of individuals can secure. All but the last group of low-ability individuals participate in this process, and the last group is thereby branded, despite its reluctance to identify itself. So, signalling is a pervasive phenomenon in the market.

Who benefits from screening? Obviously, the high-quality individual whose income rises in consequence. In a job market with no screening, all candidates will receive a pooling contract that offers everyone a wage that corresponds to their average expected productivity. However, job seekers who can provide credible indications of high ability, in terms let's say of their educational level or college grades, can expect a differential above this wage that more than compensates for the cost of their education. How much of a differential? High-ability individuals are likely to capture the full benefits of their education in a competitive job market where competition among employers will drive their wage up to the productivity level that is signalled by their qualifications. If there is a multiplicity of ability levels, we shall have a multiplicity of contracts on offer, each with wage proportional to perceived productivity. All those of more-than-average ability gain from signalling (ignoring the costs of signalling). Signalling thus opens up the way to contracts that skim the cream from the pool of jobseekers. In contrast, the lower-than-average-quality individual loses—now that he is exposed, his income drops below what he would have received if believed to be of average quality.

The system of higher education owes its existence largely to the signalling requirements of more capable workers who would like to persuade employers of their superior ability. However, colleges do more than conduct aptitude tests like SAT or GRE, or so one hopes. Perhaps they don't just help to measure productivity, they actually add to it through the propagation of knowledge. Even if they do not increase or transmit knowledge, their testing function itself might increase productivity. When individuals work in teams, the output of the team frequently depends on the configuration of abilities in the team—for example, the pace of work in the team is often limited by the ability of the slowest member, so that a more homogeneous team may produce more than a heterogeneous one. Reliable information about individual abilities facilitates more efficient assignment of individuals to teams.

Monitoring and Firing Lemons

Ability, of course, is not the only determinant of productivity. Equally important is the willingness to work and that, in turn, depends on whether one receives the fruits of one's efforts. In family enterprises, the incentive to work is strong and sustained, but an external monitor is needed elsewhere. Monitoring costs vary between products and operations.

Where output is immediate, measurable and traceable to a particular individual, monitoring is simple; payment can be linked to output through piece rates in order to maximize incentives. Harvesting is an excellent example. In highly mechanized assembly-line operations, on the other hand, machinery sets the pace of work, but errors can generally be traced to particular individuals so that monitoring is again simplified and incentives easy to sustain.

In agriculture, there is a major difference in monitoring costs between field cultivation of annual or seasonal crops and the plantation of perennials. In field agriculture, a long gestation lag separates operations like sowing, irrigation or manuring and the emergence of the final product. Most of these operations involve team effort and the vagaries of the weather play a crucial part in determining the outcome. Thus, it is almost impossible to isolate the contribution of any individual to final output. So, monitoring cannot be output-based. Since agriculture is a highly dispersed activity, it is prohibitively expensive to monitor work input as well. As a consequence, capitalist agriculture based on hired wage labour is highly inefficient in the cultivation of annuals like foodgrains, except, of course, in the harvesting phase. Family farms are much more productive.

High monitoring cost, the factor that renders capitalist cereal cultivation ineffective, also reduces the productivity of cooperative or collective farming. The major economic failure of socialism was agricultural stagnation due to the snapping of the link between effort and reward. The 10 million deaths that followed Stalin's collectivization of Soviet agriculture, the catastrophic famine that accompanied Maoist China's 'great leap forward' into the world of communes and the spectacular surge of agricultural growth initiated by Deng's virtual dissolution of communes in 1978–84, all attest to this fact. In sharp contrast, Stalin's greatest economic achievement lay in heavy basic industries where mass production of homogeneous products through mechanization and assembly-line techniques hugely simplified labour monitoring.

For most plantation crops, on the other hand, once the bushes have been planted, they require relatively little labour for maintenance. The major labour requirement is for harvesting, which is easy to monitor. Therefore, plantations are eminently suitable for large-scale capitalist agriculture. By the same token, they have also in the past been the breeding grounds of slavery. The vineyards and olive groves of ancient Greece and Rome, and the cotton, tobacco and sugar plantations of the US South and the Caribbean represented the locus classicus of the slave economy. Indentured labour systems—the successors to slavery—flourished, and still do, in the tea gardens of north-east India, the sugar plantations of Mauritius and Fiji, and the rubber plantations of Malaysia. Indeed, one of the most illuminating explanations of the American Civil War focuses on the conflict of interest between the slave-based plantation economy of the southern states and the family farms of eastern and mid-western cereal cultivators and their urban industrial allies.

In the modern factory, production processes are too complex and too bound up in interdependent team work for output-based monitoring (except in the case of assembly lines) and piece-rate wages. The entrepreneur must monitor input. But on the factory floor, he can only sporadically and imperfectly monitor the efforts of his workers, tempting the less conscientious to shirk while the more conscientious are discouraged and may leave since they are not rewarded for their exertions. The employer's reaction: higher-than-market wage offers, coupled with a strict threat of dismissal if detected shirking. The offered wage must be high enough to deter the individual from risking dismissal by shirking. This eliminates, or at least diminishes, both the incentive to shirk and the incentive to leave. Unfortunately, that is not the end of the story. If all employers offer higher-than-market wages to deter shirking, the market wage itself rises. In a full-employment economy, this makes dismissal a rather empty threat since quick re-employment is assured at a high wage. The entrepreneur who wishes to discourage shirking is then compelled to raise wages even higher. The process continues until wages rise to levels where the employers cannot afford to employ the entire workforce. Unemployment rears its ugly head. The unemployed will not be hired even if they offer to work for a lower wage since their offer will not be credible. The employer will believe that they intend to shirk since they are offering to work for a wage below the minimum that he considers necessary to deter shirking. The lemons problem is at the root of large-scale involuntary unemployment.[10]

SUMMARY

While the competitive price system minimizes information requirements, it fails to convey to the individual decision-makers crucial pieces of information, chiefly related to unobservable aspects of quality. This leads to information

---

[10] Carl Shapiro and Joseph Stiglitz, 'Equilibrium Unemployment as a Worker Discipline Device', *The American Economic Review* 74 (1984): 433–4.

asymmetry between the two sides of the market, between buyers and sellers. It tempts the informed party to cheat on quality (moral hazard). It also induces the high-quality individual who cannot earn a quality premium to exit (adverse selection). Both processes reduce the average quality in the market and induce the uninformed party to offer a lower price, which, in turn, intensify moral hazard and adverse selection and so on in a vicious circle that may lead to the breakdown and disappearance of the market.

This is a possibility that affects all markets—for products, credit, insurance, technology and labour. In order to avert, or at least minimize it, the market has developed a variety of contracts and institutions—lending on the basis of collateral or group-liability, fixed-wage and share-cropping contracts, hierarchical firms, deductible requirements in insurance, screening contracts, technology transfer through foreign direct investment, higher education as a signal of quality to employers, family farming in cereal cultivation as against capitalist farming in plantation crops, and many others. Each of these has its costs, extending from large-scale involuntary unemployment to the withdrawal of resources from directly productive activity into measures designed solely to alleviate the lemons problem, all of which one must reckon among the costs of running the market.

None of this, however, creates a presumption in favour of central planning, which remains equally, indeed possibly more, vulnerable to asymmetric information issues.

PROBLEMS

1. The Academic Council of PKU believed that invigilation in examinations was a bourgeois conspiracy and

abolished it. The students were initially delighted, but not for long. What do you think happened?

2. Farm studies in India in the 1950s and 1960s showed that small peasant farms have higher productivity per acre. In the 1970s and 1980s, after the Green Revolution, this relationship disappeared. Explain both the initial and the later findings.

3. Why don't insurance companies insure firms against loss?

4. Mass suicides by farmers whose crops have failed are a common feature of Indian agriculture. One would imagine that a large market exists for crop insurance. Why doesn't it happen? Consider both general insurance against a poor harvest and specific insurance against events like drought and pest epidemics.

5. A firm needs to invest in the initial training of its workers. Once trained, the worker may either leave the firm or stay the duration of his working life. If he leaves, the firm loses its investment in his training. However, if he stays, it more than recovers his training cost. How should the firm structure the wages it offers him? Compare its wage schedule with that of another firm that has no training requirements.

Chapter 3

Equilibrium

The price system coordinates the activities of buyers and sellers in the market to establish order amidst potential chaos. The economic counterpart of the concept of 'order' is 'equilibrium'. Equilibrium has two interrelated meanings:

1. A situation in which no one has any incentive to change anything he is doing.
2. One in which, given the existing price, everyone gets exactly what he wants.

No one has any incentive to do anything else because everyone is already doing the best for himself, given the limits set by circumstances that he cannot control (e.g. prices).

Equilibrium also means a balance of forces pulling in different directions. In the market, it means that the quantity that buyers want to buy at the ruling price exactly balances the quantity that sellers want to sell. The equilibrium price is

48

that at which quantity demanded precisely matches quantity supplied. It is the point at which the upward pressure on price from buyers just offsets the downward pressure from sellers.

Fig. 3.1

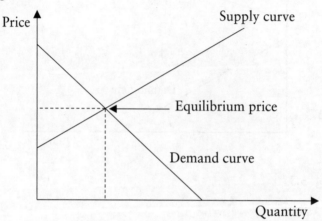

In Fig. 3.1, the two curves show the quantities that people wish to buy (demand) and sell (supply) at different prices. We have *assumed* that the demand curve slopes downward and the supply curve upward (meaning that people wish to buy more when the price is low and sell more when it is high). While this is reasonable in general, the precise proof (with possible exceptions) will be given in a later chapter.

EXISTENCE AND UNIQUENESS OF EQUILIBRIUM

At the intersection of the two curves, the quantity demanded will exactly equal the quantity supplied, defining the equilibrium price. Equilibrium exists if and only if the curves intersect. They may not.

Fig. 3.2

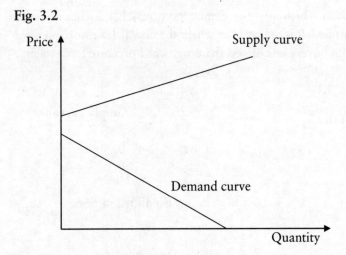

Fig. 3.3

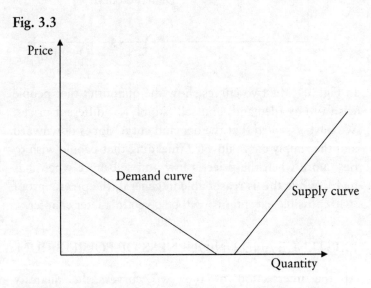

In Fig. 3.2, the most that people are prepared to offer for the good is lower than the least at which anyone is willing to supply the good, so the good will not be supplied at all.

In Fig. 3.3, the quantity demanded even when the price is zero is less than the quantity supplied at this price. The good will be a free good.

If the curves intersect, their assumed shapes guarantee that there will be only one intersection. The equilibrium, if it *exists*, will be *unique*.

CONSUMER AND PRODUCER SURPLUS

Equilibrium implies that people on both sides of the market get what they want at the current market price. But in a competitive market, it has other major implications. To understand these, we need a measure of people's willingness to buy or sell. In Fig. 3.4, AC represents a demand curve and the lengths OC_1, C_1C_2, C_2C_3 . . . represent successive small quantities of the product. The demand curve shows that, for the initial amount OC_1, the consumer is willing to pay the price C_1D_1, implying a total payment represented by the area of the little rectangle, $A_1C_1D_1O$. Similarly, for the next amount D_1D_2, he is willing to pay the area of the adjacent little rectangle, and so on. For the entire amount OD, he is willing to pay the sum of all these little rectangles. These add up to the area under the demand curve ACDO, except for the little triangles on top of our little rectangles. Now, if we make the quantities OC_1, C_1C_2, C_2C_3 . . . smaller, the little triangles diminish in size; in the limit, they disappear completely, so that the consumer's willingness to pay is well-approximated by the area under the demand curve. We could do a similar exercise with the supply curve to show that the payment that the seller needs to supply a given quantity is measurable by the area under the supply curve up to that quantity.

Fig. 3.4

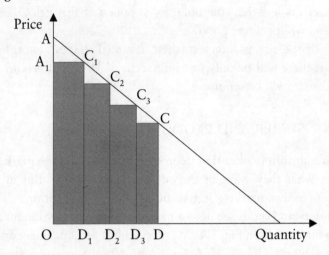

Fig. 3.5

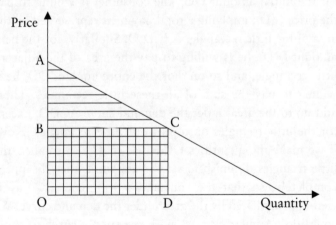

The area under the demand curve (ACDO in Fig. 3.5) then
represents the maximum that consumers are prepared to pay
for an amount OD of the good (if the alternative is to get

nothing at all). However, in a market where they can choose how much to buy at a fixed price, they can get OD by paying a total of BCDO (market price into quantity bought). Thus, access to the market gives buyers a *consumers' surplus* of ABC.

Similarly, the area under the supply curve (ABDO in Fig. 3.6) is the minimum that suppliers need if they are to bring a quantity OD into the market. The market, however, offers them the larger amount OCBD, which includes a *producer's surplus* of ABC.

Fig. 3.6

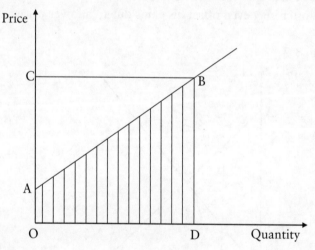

Market equilibrium maximizes the sum of consumers' and producers' surpluses. In particular, at the equilibrium, this sum will be larger than when government creates a disequilibrium by decreeing that a good must be sold below market price (as in food price control). In Fig. 3.7, the down-sloping demand curve and the up-sloping supply curve intersect at the equilibrium C, generating a consumer's surplus ACE and a producer's surplus RCE, adding up to the sum ACR. However, if the government sets a lower-than-equilibrium price OF (as against the equilibrium price OE), the quantity supplied will contract from OD to OH. The consumer's surplus will now be the area AFGJ, while the producer's surplus falls to the triangle RFG. As a result of price control, the sum of the two diminishes by the area JCG. The producer is unambiguously worse off. It is not even clear that the consumer is better off since we cannot assert with certainty that the area AFGJ is any larger than the area ACE. The consumer's losses due to the smaller quantity on offer may even offset his gains due to a lower price.

Fig. 3.7

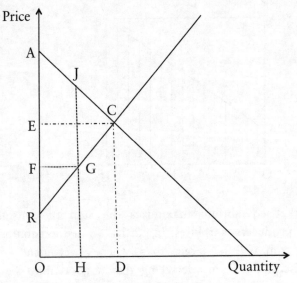

Similarly, if the government dictates a higher-than-equilibrium price (as in minimum-wage laws), the consequence is a decline in the total surplus of employers and employees. Employers lose unambiguously. Whether employees gain or lose depends on whether their losses due to lower employment are compensated by their gains due to higher wages.

In both cases, however, the decrease in total surplus means that the gains of the gainers, if any, are less than the losses of the losers. There is no way that the gainers can compensate the losers, even if they want to.

All this, of course, assumes that the policies can be implemented successfully and free of cost. However, disequilibrium by government fiat is always difficult and costly to sustain. Selling below the equilibrium price or hiring above the equilibrium wage implies excess demand for goods or excess supply of jobseekers. This means queues and waiting. One pays in waiting time for a lower-than-equilibrium price or a higher-than-equilibrium wage. Every Indian who remembers life before the 1991 reforms and every survivor of the Soviet Union before 1989 will recall the pervasiveness of queues and the many anecdotes that they gave rise to.[11] One queued up at ration shops

---

[11] Possibly the most famous of these, a story that attests not only to the length of queues but also to the devotion of the Russian people to their national icons, relates the ordeal of a member of the Siberian Inouit tribe who went on a trip to Moscow during a period of drastic scarcity of vodka. On the eve of his trip, he was asked by his village headman to get him a couple of bottles of vodka from the capital. 'But where would I find the vodka?' asked the troubled tribesman. 'Just look around,' explained the headman, 'and join the longest queue.' In due time, the tribesman returned, but without the vodka. 'What happened?'

for hours if the cost of waiting was less than one's savings from buying from the ration shop; if it was greater, one hired local urchins to do the waiting. The urchins, in turn, set up their own private markets, bargaining with those behind them to interchange places for a consideration. The cost to the final consumer was often driven up close to the maximum he would have voluntarily paid in an open market, but the benefit of the higher de facto prices went not to the supplier but was either dissipated in costly waiting or captured by intermediaries (like our urchins).

Further, price controls and minimum wages generate incentives on both sides of the market for evasion. With prices controlled and quantities therefore rationed, the buyer is willing to pay, and seller eager to accept, a higher price for a larger quantity. Neither has any interest to report the misdemeanour. So, a parallel economy flourishes in happy coexistence with such price controls. India's black markets in every price-controlled product are the stuff of legends. There is a story of the enterprising 1970's garbage collector who bought used bags from the Cement Corporation of India and the Fertilizer Corporation of India, set his numerous and not-quite-as-enterprising family to shake them out and made a fortune selling the residual cement and fertilizer at black-market prices. And visitors to the Soviet Union before its dissolution will recall being stalked by desperadoes pleading pathetically

---

demanded the headman. 'Well,' replied the native, 'I did join the longest queue, but when I got to the head of the line, the bartender was dead.' He had, of course, joined the queue in front of Lenin's mausoleum.

for one's dollars in exchange for roubles at many times the official rate.

Moreover, the government's efforts to enforce such controls and private individuals' efforts to conceal their evasion both absorb resources, which must be withdrawn from productive work, thus adding to the costs directly imposed by the disequilibrium prices themselves. Very similar are the costs imposed by minimum-wage legislation.

Finally, wherever the quality of a product is unverifiable by third parties and, therefore, not legally enforceable, price controls create a strong incentive for the supplier to dilute quality. It is costly to achieve quality and, in a situation of excess demand created by prices below equilibrium, the competitive pressure for high quality disappears. The socialist world was notable for the production of low-quality, price-controlled goods for mass consumption—soap, for example. Visitors to many socialist countries who made the mistake of using the local soap often emerged from their baths smelling so strongly of pineapple or cucumber that the local insect population promptly made a beeline for them in the belief that a free meal was on offer.

Why do governments follow such expensive policies? Part of the answer lies in distributional considerations. Lower prices *may* benefit consumers more than smaller quantities hurt them. Higher wages *may* benefit workers despite the accompanying loss of employment. Even if they do not, the very fact that producers and employers are undeniably hurt (by lower prices for their products and higher wage costs) may create the illusion among consumers and workers (who constitute far larger constituencies) of a caring, redistributive government.

Is there a better option? If redistribution is the government's objective, this could probably be better accomplished through direct taxes and expenditures than through disequilibrium pricing. Of course, taxation of income and subsidies for consumption would impair the incentives to work and earn (why work hard when the government will tax your added earnings and pay for your extra consumption?), but so would any kind of redistribution. The direct tax method at least minimizes the excess burden—the additional costs that result from distortion of the price system. The fact that governments still often choose the latter route is probably due to a belief in the existence of a *fiscal illusion*: keen popular awareness of, and resistance to any increase in income taxes coupled with relative ignorance of the largely incommensurable burdens imposed by indirect tax and meddling by administrative fiat with the price system.

The government, however, is only one of the possible sources of disequilibrium pricing. Job discrimination against members of specific groups on the grounds of colour, caste or gender is another example. Consider Fig. 3.8, where the demand for a particular variety of skilled labour is given by the demand curve AFC. The supply of labour has two components—a white (or upper caste) component reflected by the supply curve HF and a black (or lower caste) element. Total labour supply is the sum of the two and is represented by the aggregate labour supply curve JC. The equilibrium price is CD determined by the intersection of the aggregate supply and demand curves for labour. If, however, prejudice restricts employment only to whites (or upper-caste individuals), the relevant labour supply is given by the curve HF; wage then rises to PG and employment contacts to a purely white (upper caste) component EF. White (upper caste) labour is now better off—not only has its wage risen, its employment has also expanded from BK to EF, resulting in an increase in its surplus from BKH to EFH. However, the employer's surplus has diminished as a consequence of the rise in wage from ABC to AEF. The market, therefore, creates a strong incentive for collusion between employers and black (lower caste) labour and the breakdown of the colour (or caste) bar. Not only will employers who defect from the all-white (upper caste) coalition enjoy higher profits, they could also drive members of the coalition out of the market, unless, of course, state policy (such as apartheid) or coercion by the beneficiaries of the colour (or caste) bar are employed against defectors.

The levelling effect of the market, its erosive impact on discrimination, may not work where productivity is primarily the product of costly training. Here, job discrimination may discourage the group that is discriminated against from investing in training, thereby holding its productivity down and confirming the stereotypical belief that it is incompetent as a group. Alternatively, members of this group may simply apply themselves less to their jobs since they expect to be rewarded less by employers who discriminate against them, thus conforming to the stereotype of laziness and inefficiency. Stereotyping could be the source of a self-perpetuating wage gap based on gender, race or caste unrelated to innate efficiency. However, if stereotyping is not universal, the market is likely to erode such wage differentials. The employers who do not discriminate would establish a reputation that attracts capable and aspiring employees from the groups discriminated against, earn higher profits than employers who do discriminate, expand and ultimately drive the latter out of the market.

Fig. 3.8

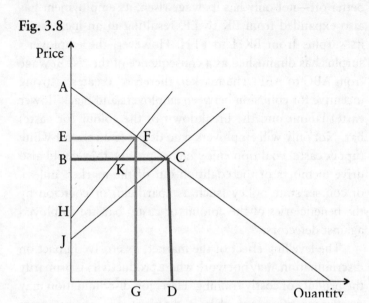

OTHER CONCEPTS OF EQUILIBRIUM

The notion of equilibrium we have used in this and previous chapters refers to a state where people are doing the best that they can do for themselves under the prices ruling in the market. This is appropriate when individuals take prices as given. One must adapt to what one cannot change. There are, however, other possible circumstances and alternative concepts of equilibrium as well. The best known of these is the concept invented by John Nash,[12] the

---

[12] John Nash, 'Equilibrium Points in N-person Games', *Proceedings of the National Academy of Sciences* 36 (1950): 48–9.

Nobel prize-winning mathematician and protagonist of the movie *A Beautiful Mind*. In *Nash equilibrium*, everyone does the best for himself, given what everyone else is doing. Nash equilibrium resembles competitive equilibrium in that, if once reached, it is self-perpetuating, unless the various parties collude. No unilateral deviation is profitable, so none will occur. On the other hand, in Nash equilibrium, agents can manipulate prices: they do not take prices as parameters. This is a concept to which we shall return to later.

PARAMETERS OF DEMAND AND SUPPLY

A tale that is almost certainly untrue but often retailed to freshmen students of economics is of a US President who, after being elected on a platform of balanced budgets and price stability, promptly produced the largest peacetime deficit budget in US history. When a journalist at his next press conference asked, 'But what about inflation?', President X supposedly replied, 'I don't understand all this talk about inflation. Every freshman student of economics knows that when prices go up, demand falls. But when demand falls, prices must come down again. Inflation is impossible.'

The presidential paradox juxtaposes two propositions, both indisputably true:

1. When prices go up, demand falls.
2. When demand falls, prices come down.

If the words in the two statements have the same meanings, they can indeed be linked and the president's logic is ironclad. Inflation is impossible. Yet, as every freshman student, and not only of economics, knows, prices do go up and stay up. Inflation does occur.

To resolve this mystery, one must look a little deeper into the foundations on which demand and supply curves are constructed. These curves depict the relationship between quantities demanded and supplied on the one hand and price on the other. However, quantities demanded depend not only on the price of the good but also on tastes, income and other prices (notably of substitutes and complements). These may be called the *parameters of the demand curve.* As they change, the demand curve shifts bodily. Such shifts in the demand curve itself are distinguishable from shifts along the demand curve (when quantity demanded changes due to price change only with the parameters of the curve remaining constant). Similarly, the parameters of supply include not only weather and security but also technology, the prices of productive inputs and the prices of other outputs (which determine the profitability of producing this particular good rather than other goods). Changes in these parameters shift the supply curve.

Demand and supply curves are not actually observable in the market. One sees only the price and the quantity traded at a particular moment (the point of intersection of the existing demand and supply curves). Over a period of time, we observe a time series of such intersections: we cannot tell immediately whether this time path represents a demand curve (which it would if only the supply curve had shifted) or a supply curve (if only the demand curve had shifted) or neither (if both had shifted). This is known as the *identification problem.* To solve this problem, we have to look at the parameters of supply and demand and check which of them had changed in the meanwhile.

STABILITY OF EQUILIBRIUM

An important aspect of equilibrium is its stability—the ability of the system to return to its initial state after a disturbance. This is a property of the dynamic process of adjustment which is set in motion after the system has been knocked out of equilibrium. In the market, the common assumption is that, in disequilibrium, it is the price that adjusts, rising when demand exceeds supply and falling when supply exceeds demand. With price adjusting and the standard upward-sloping supply curve and downward-sloping demand curve, the market will always be stable (why? Check this for yourself).

However, demand and supply curves need not have such shapes. Then, the stability of equilibrium is not guaranteed. For example, if both demand and supply curves slope down with the demand curve sloping down more steeply, any disequilibrium will progressively increase and the market will move further and further from its initial position (check why this happens).

The previous paragraph assumed that the market responds to disequilibrium by adjusting prices, a process described as Walrasian after the great nineteenth-century economist Leon Walras.[13] The equally great Cambridge economist Alfred Marshall proposed an alternative adjustment mechanism.[14] He suggested quantity adjustment—if the price that buyers are prepared to offer for a given quantity (*demand price*)

---

[13] Leon Walras, *Elements of Pure Economics,* trans. W. Jaffe (London: Allen & Unwin, 1926).

[14] Alfred Marshall, *Principles of Economics* (London: Macmillan, 1920).

exceeds the price that sellers require to supply it (*supply price*), sellers will offer larger quantities, and buyers, too, will buy more. The two adjustment processes have different implications for stability. With traditional down-sloping demand curves and up-sloping supply curves, equilibrium will always be both Walras-stable and Marshall-stable. But with different shapes of the supply and demand curves, the conditions for Walras stability and Marshall stability diverge. Thus, if both curves slope downward, the market will be Walras-unstable but Marshall-stable if the demand curve slopes down more steeply and Walras-stable but Marshall-unstable in the reverse eventuality. The nature of the adjustment mechanism in a particular market matters.

An unstable market results in disorder. For example, if the food market is unstable, food price could explode, resulting in famine. So the shapes of the demand and supply curves are crucial determinants of the ability of the price system to perform its function of bringing order to the potential chaos of an unregulated economy, and it is to a study of these shapes that we must now turn.

SUMMARY

The economist's conception of order is the notion of equilibrium, a state in which no one wants to do anything different from what he has been doing because he is already doing the best he can, given the circumstances that are beyond his control. In the competitive market, prices are beyond the individual's control. So, the notion of equilibrium requires that the quantity of any good that buyers want to buy at the current price precisely equals the quantity that sellers want to sell. This requirement is fulfilled at the intersection of the demand and supply curves for the good.

In equilibrium, the sum of the consumer's and producer's surplus (the benefit derived by the buyer or the seller from being able to buy what they want at the market price) is maximized. Disequilibria, such as those sustained by government fiat, result in a loss of surplus. They also create incentives for evasion of such fiats and lead to withdrawal of resources from productive work, whether in order to enforce such fiats or to evade them. Other kinds of disequilibrium (such as job discrimination on the basis of caste, colour or gender) may be sustained not by coercive authority but by social pressure—in such cases, the market tends generally to undermine discrimination.

The demand and supply curves portray the relationship between prices and quantities demanded or supplied. However, the curves may shift due to changes in their underlying parameters—chiefly tastes, income and other prices for the demand curve, and technology and prices of inputs and other outputs for the supply curve. Such shifts induce changes in equilibria. It is important to distinguish between shifts along a demand or supply curve and shifts of the curves themselves in order to avoid logical fallacies.

With conventional down-sloping demand and up-sloping supply curves, an equilibrium may or may not exist, but if it does, it will be unique and stable. With less conventional shapes, instability is possible, but the conditions for stability vary according to whether the market adjusts to disequilibrium by changing prices or quantities.

PROBLEMS

1. The price of oil is rising, but two economists, Prof. Know All and Dr Too Smart, disagree about the causes. While Prof. Know All attributes it to the improvement in the American economy, Dr Too Smart blames it on the war in the Middle East and consequent disruption in oil supply. Assuming that these are the only possible explanations, devise a simple test to distinguish between the two.

2. The sugarcane harvest in Illyria has failed.

   a) Use supply-and-demand analysis to predict the consequences for the price and quantity of sugar.

   b) Prof. Know All recommends that government should impose a ceiling on sugar prices to take care of the situation. What in your opinion would be the results of this policy?

   c) Dr Too Smart, on the other hand, feels that a floor should be set to sugar prices to protect the interests of sugar producers. What do you think this would imply?

Chapter 4

The Consumer

The market is a place where buyers and sellers, consumers and producers meet and interact. Generally they do so in ways readily understood by common sense. When, however, we look more closely, we are immediately confronted by a bewildering box of puzzles. To cite just a few:

1. Consumers generally buy more of any good when it is priced lower; but why, in some exceptional cases, notably of basic foods, is this relationship reversed?
2. Why are producers of some goods delighted at the advent of a recession?
3. Why are drug dealers deeply distressed when their drugs are legalized?
4. Why don't bars, telephone companies and electricity suppliers charge fixed prices based on consumption? Why instead do these very different kinds of business share the strange common feature of a two-part pricing system?

5. Governments often claim on the basis of their measures that national income and output rates are booming at unprecedented rates. Economists hostile to the ruling dispensation often use the same raw data but different measures to assert that the economy is stagnant or contracting. How do they do it?

6. Generally, high-wage individuals work harder (though this is not universally true). But when all wages rise, the average number of hours worked generally declines. Why?

7. As wages rise, people can afford more children. Why instead do they have fewer?

To understand the mental processes behind such individual decisions, we must begin with an assumption about the consumer's psyche: we postulate that the consumer is *rational*. Rationality implies that the consumer can decide between any pair of alternatives—his preferences are *complete*. It also means that his preferences are:

1. *Consistent*: If he prefers X to Y, he does not simultaneously prefer Y to X.

2. *Transitive*: If he prefers X to Y and Y to Z, he prefers X to Z; while if he is indifferent between X and Y and between Y and Z, he is indifferent between X and Z.

Rationality is a strong assumption. Modern psychology does not portray man as a dispassionate maximizer, coolly calculating the pros and cons of all his decisions with judicial calm. He is, in fact, a bundle of conflicting instincts on which a superficial order has been imposed by the learning processes of real life. But beneath the surface, explosive subconscious impulses simmer, ready to erupt at the touch of experience in ways that have nothing to do with preexisting preferences. To understand the implications of this, consider a drug addict; he craves his drug, but he also fears what it may do to him in the long, possibly even the short, run. He is unable to resolve this contradiction. To describe him as a consistent decision-maker would be a travesty of facts. More generally, there is the contradiction between temptation and self-control. My health dictates the strictest of diets, but the mouth-watering advertisement of a double cheeseburger with extra-large fries is hammering at the gates of my resistance. Is this a situation that can be aptly described in terms of the cold calculus of maximization? The chief value of the rationality postulate is instrumental—it enables us to make definite predictions about behaviour, while if we permit irrationality, anything goes. However, recent findings in behavioural economics show the importance of specific kinds of non-rational behaviour and have led to the relaxation of the assumption of full rationality in some specific ways. Later in this chapter, we will touch briefly upon some of these specific modifications of full rationality and their implications. For the present, however, we retain the assumption of full rationality.

A rational consumer can rank alternatives in what is described as a *preference ordering*. Preference orderings can be of two kinds. The first kind is *lexicographic,* like the words in a dictionary. Just as each word in a dictionary has its own separate place, in a lexicographic ordering, no two alternatives can share the same rank. When the consumer faces two distinct baskets of goods, he must value them differently; less of one good can never be compensated by more of another. Lexicographic orderings do not permit substitution. They are a list of rigid priorities. Honesty, for example, may be my top priority, from which I will not deviate regardless of the amount of money I am offered for doing so. Most orderings, however, are non-lexicographic. Consumers often find different baskets of goods equally satisfactory, less of one good having been compensated by more of another. They are *indifferent* between these baskets. In a graph where different quantities of two goods, X and Y, are measured along the axes, each basket corresponds to a different point (a different combination of X and Y). The locus of all points that are equally satisfactory to the consumer is called an *indifference curve*. For a complete non-lexicographic ordering, every possible commodity basket (every point on our graph) will lie on some indifference curve and its ranking relative to some other basket will reveal which of the indifference curves through the two points represents a higher level of satisfaction.

Indifference curves are a picture of the consumer's preferences and represent as such a major analytical tool. However, we need to make some additional psychological assumptions to define their geometry if we are to derive some meaningful conclusions.

INDIFFERENCE CURVES

A rational consumer has consistent and transitive preferences. For preference orderings that are rational and non-lexicographic, we make two standard assumptions about the consumer's tastes:

1. Non-satiation: The consumer never wants less of any good and generally wants more. This implies that indifference curves further to the north-east correspond to higher levels of satisfaction. It also means that indifference curves slope downward to the right, reflecting a process of compensation as the loss due to less of one good is just offset by more of another. This *negative slope* measures the substitutability of one good

for another and is called the *marginal rate of substitution* (MRS) between them.

2. Preference for variety: If the consumer is indifferent between two baskets of goods, he will prefer a basket that is intermediate between them to either. In geometric terms, if two points lie on the same indifference curve, any point on the line segment joining them must lie on a higher indifference curve. This implies that indifference curves are convex to the origin (or equivalently, that the MRS of X for Y diminishes as the quantity of X increases and that of Y falls).

Extreme kinds of preference result in special shapes of indifference curves: *perfect substitutability* between X and Y results in linear indifference curves (Fig. 4.1).

Fig. 4.1

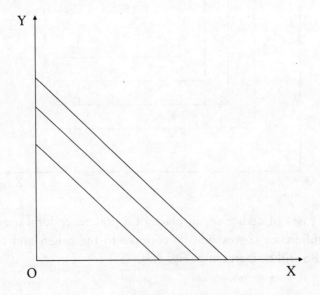

Perfect complementarity implies L-shaped indifference curves with the kink indicating the fixed proportions in which X and Y are consumed (Fig. 4.2). An example would be the relationship between left shoes and right. This is also the only exception to the rule that consumers want more of any good. Given the fixed proportions in which the different goods are used, any excess of one good is useless. However, as long as disposal of the excess is free, the consumer is indifferent between just the right proportions and an excess of one good. Indifference curves exist, even though with shapes different from the standard downward slope.

Fig. 4.2

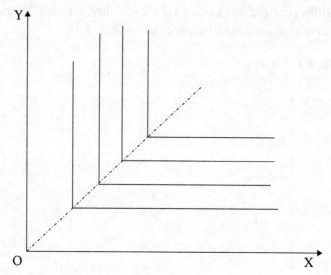

In cases of addiction, in place of a preference for variety, indifference curves will be concave to the origin and the MRS will be increasing (Fig. 4.3).

Fig. 4.3

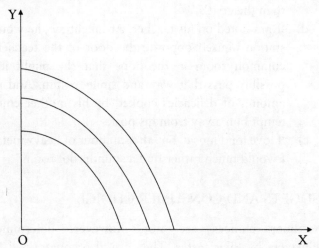

The reader may test his understanding of the principles developed in this chapter by solving the problems posed below.

PROBLEMS

1. Each of the following statements tells us something about an indifference map. What do they say in each case?
   a) 'Every man has his price.' (Henry Ford)
   b) 'I don't care whether the cat is black or white as long as it catches mice.' (Deng Xiao Ping)
   c) 'Hameed, the great Indian wrestler, was very particular about his diet. Dinner for him meant one full goat cooked in one kilo of butter with precisely forty chapatis. The slightest deviation from these

proportions and the cook's fate would be worse
than the goat's.'

d) 'Ram doted on his teacher. At lunchtime, he would
station himself opposite the door of the teacher's
common room in the hope that she might just
possibly pass that way and smile at him. And no
amount of delicacies cooked by his mother could
tempt him away from his post.'

e) 'I love loud music. But after an hour of heavy metal,
I would much rather find a soundproof room.'

BUDGETS AND CONSUMER CHOICE

Consumer choices are not, however, determined
exclusively by their tastes. They are also constrained by
their budgets. Given a fixed budget and fixed prices over
which he has no control, the consumer can only buy those
baskets of goods that lie in the budget set—the triangular
area bounded by the X- and Y-axes and the *budget line*,
the locus of all combinations of purchases that exhaust
the budget (Fig. 4.4). The slope of the budget line is the
ratio of the prices of X and Y (P_x/P_y): since these prices are
fixed, so is the slope (i.e. the budget line is linear, rather
than curved).

The consumer will choose that point on the budget set
that takes him to the highest possible indifference curve.
With standard indifference curves, this will be the point
of tangency A between the budget line and an indifference
curve, which, under these assumptions, will be unique.
At this point, the slopes of the indifference curve and the
budget line are equal: MRS = P_x/P_y.

Fig. 4.4

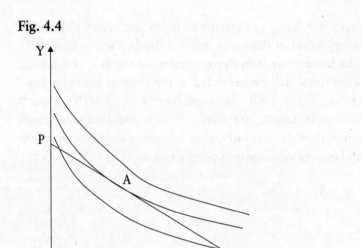

INCOME EFFECTS

If the budget increases, with prices constant, the budget line shifts upward with constant slope (Fig. 4.5).

After such a parallel shift, there will be a new tangency point B and a new consumption pattern. This shift is an *income effect*. It affects the demand for different goods differently. The income effect on the demand for X is reflected by the *income-elasticity of demand* for X—the percentage change in demand for X due to 1 per cent change in income. The income elasticity is positive for normal goods, but there do exist *inferior goods* for which it is negative. As their incomes rose, Indian consumers, for example, bought less of the coarser foodgrains—millets like ragi, jowar and bajra—at least until medical research revealed their health benefits. Changes in tastes and technology often change the composition of the set of inferior goods. Pure cotton cloth, which was once considered inferior (in the face of synthetic substitutes), is now regarded as the stuff of haute couture. On the other hand, the availability of high-tech products has made radios, standard bicycles and kerosene lamps inferior goods. It is only when economic contraction sets in and incomes decline that people buy more of such products.

Fig. 4.5

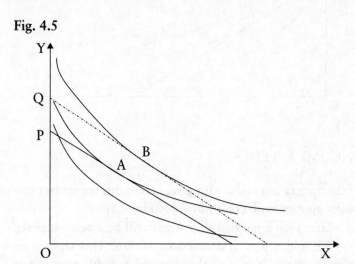

If the income-elasticity of demand for X is not only positive but also higher than 1, the demand for X rises faster than income. A 1 per cent rise in income increases demand for X by more than 1 per cent. According to *Engel's Law*, a well-known empirical generalization, manufactures as a group have an income elasticity higher than 1 while agricultural products have an income elasticity less than 1 as a group (not, however, for all agricultural goods, as some are regarded as luxuries whose consumption rises faster than income).

A consequence of Engel's Law is that the world as a whole must industrialize as its income rises (since the output of manufactures must rise faster than income in order to match the changing pattern of demand). However, this is only true of a closed economy (such as the world at large) which must produce all it consumes. An open, trading economy can have a production pattern very different from its consumption pattern. Some high-income countries remain major primary producers on the basis of their large-scale export of primary products—Denmark, for example, on the basis of ham and butter, New Zealand on the basis of lamb and dairy products, and Australia on the basis of wool, meat and minerals.

PRICE EFFECTS

If, however, the price of X falls with income constant, the budget line rotates about its intercept on the Y-axis, with its slope (= P_x/P_y) now lower, since P_x is smaller (Fig. 4.6).

Fig. 4.6

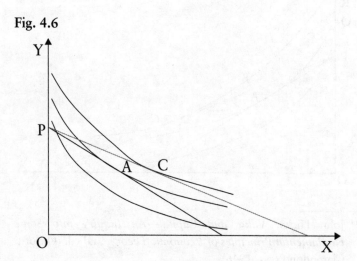

The movement to a new tangency point C is the *price effect*. This can be decomposed into two components (Fig. 4.7):

1. An income effect component (the movement from A to B): the fall in one price increases the purchasing power of money income, it amounts to a rise in income of PQ and affects demand for X and Y according to their income elasticities.
2. A substitution effect component (the movement from B to C): the fall in the relative price of X induces the substitution of the now-cheaper good X for the dearer good Y.

Such a decomposition is known as the Hicks decomposition.[15]

Fig. 4.7

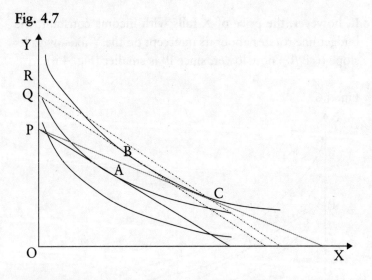

---

[15] John Hicks, *Value and Capital: An Inquiry into Some Fundamental Principles of Economic Theory*, 2nd ed. (Oxford: Clarendon Press, 1946).

An alternative way of decomposing the price effect is known as the Slutsky decomposition.[16] It divides the price effect into:

1. A change in income (from OP to OR) just enough to enable the consumer to buy the new basket of goods C at the old price, represented by a parallel shift of the old budget line to a level that just passes through C.
2. A movement along this new budget line through R and C to the point where the slope of an indifference curve is just equal to the new price (which is the point C itself).

A price change induces a change in consumption pattern. An income change that would have enabled the consumer to buy the new basket of goods at the old prices is the Slutsky income effect. An income change that would, at the old prices, have made the consumer just as well off as he now is represents the Hicks income effect. The Slutsky income effect is larger than the Hicks income effect (PR is larger than PQ).

If X is a normal (non-inferior) good, both the income effect and the substitution effect of the fall in P_x on the demand for X are positive—so, as the price of X falls, the demand for X rises—the standard shape of the demand curve. However, if X is inferior, the income effect is negative and opposite in direction to the positive substitution effect. If the income effect is both negative and large and the substitution effect is weak, the former will overcome the latter and the

---

[16] Eugen Slutsky, 'Sulla teoria del bilancio del consumatore', *Giornale degli Economisti* 51: 1–26, trans., 'On the Theory of the Budget of the Consumer', in *Readings in Price Theory*, ed. Kenneth E. Boulding and George Stigler (Illinois: Homewood, 1952), pp: 27–56.

price effect will have a wrong sign—as P_x falls, the demand for X will fall. The size of the income effect depends on two factors: the budget share of X (which determines the extent to which the fall in price of X affects purchasing power) and the marginal propensity to consume X (the fraction of any real income increase that will be spent on more X). If these two are significant (the marginal propensity to consume X being negative), and if X has few substitutes, the chances are that the net price effect will be perverse. A good of this kind, with a negative price effect, is called a *Giffen good*. Staple foods, which bulk large in the budgets of the poor, are often Giffen goods. Their budget share is large, the marginal propensity to consume them is negative and large (as income rises, their consumption diminishes sharply), and they have few substitutes. In a famine caused by food shortage, as the price of food rises, the demand for food may rise (if the food is a Giffen good), accelerating the rise in price, increasing food demand further and so on in a vicious spiral, which is one of the most troublesome features of a famine.

In the case of the vast majority of goods, however, demand falls as price rises. The economist's measure of the responsiveness of demand to price changes is the price elasticity of demand, the percentage fall in demand due to 1 per cent rise in price. A Giffen good is negatively price-elastic, since a rise in its price induces a rise in demand for it. For non-Giffen goods, a critical threshold is represented by unit price elasticity. If demand falls in exact proportion to the rise in price, the total expenditure on the good remains invariant as price changes. On the other hand, if demand is price inelastic (price elasticity of demand is less than 1), demand does not decline much as price rises, so that, to the delight of the producer, expenditures on the good (and therefore the producer's total sales revenue) increase even as his costs decline because he has to produce less. Cigarette producers, for example, earn more as cigarette prices rise: higher prices hardly discourage smokers, who have to be more effectively intimidated by horrific pictures on cigarette packs of what smoking does to their lungs. If, on the other hand, price elasticity exceeds 1, demand falls precipitously as price rises, total expenditure and—total sales revenue— contract.

Since the price effect has both a substitution and an income-effect component, a good will be highly price elastic if it has many excellent substitutes and has a high income elasticity of demand (due to a large budget share and a high marginal propensity to consume it). Luxuries have some of these characteristics—many substitutes and a high marginal propensity to consume (though not necessarily a large budget share) and tend therefore to respond flexibly to price changes. Any single producer in a competitive industry faces highly price-elastic demand due to many nearly identical substitutes—any increase in his prices induces a mass migration of his customers to his rivals. Necessities, on the other hand, have low price elasticities—they have few substitutes and are not much affected by income changes. Addictive products—cigarettes, alcohol and drugs—have similar low elasticities of demand. Producers of necessary and addictive goods benefit from sharp increases in their prices.

PROBLEMS

1. Are the following statements true or false (T or F)? If they are false, correct them:

a) If the price elasticity of demand for X is higher than 1 at all prices, the consumer buys nothing but X at very high prices of X.

b) If the income elasticity of demand for X exceeds 1 at all incomes, the consumer buys nothing but X at very high incomes.

c) All inferior goods are Giffen goods.

d) All Giffen goods are inferior.

e) A Giffen good accounts for a very small proportion of a consumer's budget.

f) If the income elasticity of demand for X exceeds 1 at all incomes, the consumer buys nothing but X at very high incomes.

g) As coffee prices rise, I drink less tea. This means that tea is an inferior good for me.

h) My demand curve for any particular good cannot possibly be upward sloping at all prices.

2. A consumer spends all his income on X and Y. Which of the following statements about his behaviour is inconsistent with consumer behaviour theory:

a) As his income rises, he buys less of X.

b) As the price of Y falls, he buys less of Y.

c) Both (a) and (b) hold simultaneously.

d) As the price of Y falls, he buys more of both X and Y.

3. Suppose the price elasticity of good X is zero. Good X is most likely to be:

a) Emergency surgery

b) A luxury yacht

c) Wheat

d) A brand of toothpaste

4. Ram has decided to spend one-third of his income on biryani. What is the income elasticity of his demand for biryani? What is his price elasticity of demand? How will these be affected if his tastes change and he decides to spend half of his income on biryani?

5. Sita buys only two goods—bread and jeans. Her income and the price of bread are constant. As jeans become costlier, she buys less bread. Which of the following does this imply:
   a) The price elasticity of demand for jeans is less than 1.
   b) Jeans are a luxury.
   c) Bread is an inferior good.
   d) There is no substitution effect in this case.

6. The price elasticity of my demand for X is less than 1. Would a rise in price of X reduce my demand both for X and for at least one other good?

7. Prof. Know All was lecturing his economics class. 'Over the years,' he thundered, 'the consumption of grain—the poor man's staple—has consistently declined, while that of fruits, vegetables, meat and other luxury foods has risen. This conclusively proves that the rich are growing richer and the poor poorer.' 'I don't agree, Prof.,' piped up Ms Smarty, who delighted in contradicting her teachers, and proceeded to explain. What do you think was her explanation?

8. I am currently spending half my income on food. Would a 50 per cent rise in the price of food, together with a 25 per cent rise in my income, leave me just as well-off?

APPLICATIONS

1. *Excess burden of indirect tax* (Fig. 4.8): Suppose OP
    is a consumer's income before tax, the slope of PA the
    initial price of good X and A, the initial consumption
    basket. Suppose further that an indirect tax is levied
    on X, raising its price to the slope of the straight line
    through PC. The new consumption basket will be C.
    Under tax, the consumption of X will drop to CT and
    the consumer will be paying an amount PT (given the
    after-tax price, represented by the slope of the line
    through PC) which includes both the seller's price and
    the tax. Since the seller's price is represented by the
    slope of PA, or of its parallel CS, the seller's receipts
    amount to ST, which leaves an amount PS as the
    government's tax revenue. However, if the government
    simply deducts an amount PQ from the consumer's
    income and does not distort prices away from their
    initial level, the consumer will be able to reach (at point
    B) the same indifference curve as under indirect tax.
    But PQ exceeds ST: income tax generates more revenue
    than indirect tax while leaving the taxpayer just as
    well-off. PQ is the Hicks income-effect component of
    the price change due to indirect tax. Alternatively, the
    government could levy an income tax of PS (equal to the
    yield of the indirect tax) without distorting prices. This
    enables the consumer to afford the same bundle C as
    under indirect tax. But since the rightward extension of
    the line SC climbs above the indifference curve through
    C, it also enables the consumer to buy a better bundle.
    PS is the Slutsky income effect.

Fig. 4.8

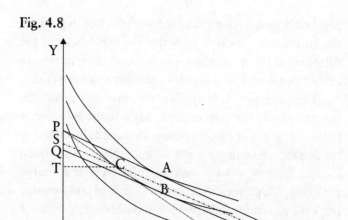

2. *Two-part pricing* (Fig. 4.9): Suppose now that the government itself is the seller of the good X. It could charge the consumer at a fixed rate per unit of X consumed (like the seller's price plus tax that he has to pay under indirect taxation). This would result in the consumer buying AS of the good and paying the government PS. However, the government could substantially increase its receipts by charging the consumer as low a price as possible (equal to the marginal cost of the good) represented by the slope of the line BQ and levying a fixed charge PQ (like an income tax) that would reduce him to the same level of satisfaction as at A. The consumer will now buy a larger amount BR of the good, paying QR for it in addition to the fixed charge PQ. Thus, two-part pricing will result in the government receiving an additional amount RS while leaving the consumer equally well-off. Here, the lower unit

price of X generates a Hicks income effect of PQ, which the government pockets. It is also the beneficiary of the substitution effect—the movement along the indifference curve from A to B which yields even more sales revenue.

The same principle applies whenever any producer, not necessarily the government, has a monopoly over a particular good. It can maximize its receipts by charging the lowest possible price per unit coupled with a fixed charge. Examples: bars with an entry fee and a charge per drink, telephones with a monthly rental and a charge per call, electricity bills with a monthly charge plus a charge per unit of power consumed. The low unit price encourages the customer to buy more of the good, while the high fixed charge diverts some of his income away from other goods to the producer who is using two-part pricing. Further, since this pricing policy yields a higher income than a flat rate, firms which use it will drive others out of the market.

Fig. 4.9

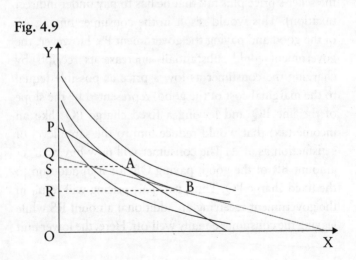

3. *Quantity indices*: Since different outputs change at different rates and even in different directions, how does one construct a composite index of output growth? Ideally, such an index should weight different goods on the basis of the relative values that people attach to them. And this is best reflected by the prices that people are prepared to pay for them. But prices change over time and there is no unanimity on which prices should be used. The Laspeyre Index compares the cost of today's basket of goods at yesterday's prices with what yesterday's basket actually cost (at the prices then ruling) to establish the rate of growth. In contrast, the Paasche Index compares the current cost of today's basket of goods with what yesterday's basket would have cost at current prices.

In constructing such indices, however, one ignores the fact that relative prices and the composition of output are not independent of each other. Changes in relative prices change the composition of the consumer's basket of purchases by inducing substitution effects— the consumer substitutes goods that are cheaper today for goods that are dearer. Thus, today's basket is dominated by goods that were high-priced yesterday but have since become cheap. So, if we measure the cost of buying today's basket of goods at yesterday's prices (as in Laspeyre's Index), we assign a relatively high weight to outputs that have increased (because their prices have fallen since yesterday) and a low weight to those that have contracted, thus imparting an upward bias to our measure of output change. On the other hand, Paasche's Index does the precise opposite. It uses current prices as weights. Thus it assigns a high weight to goods that have become costlier since yesterday and, therefore, have shrunk in volume and a low weight to those that have become cheaper and therefore more popular, thereby creating a downward bias.

The point is illustrated in Fig. 4.10. Consider the commodity baskets P and Q, chosen yesterday (at the prices represented by the budget line AB) and today (at prices represented by CD), respectively. The two lie on the same indifference curve, indicating that an accurate measure of income should indicate no change. However, if we value Q at P's prices and compare it with the value of P at P's prices, we create the illusion of an output increase by the factor OA_1/OA. If, on the other hand, we value P at Q's prices, we generate an illusory contraction by the factor OC/OC_1.

Fig. 4.10

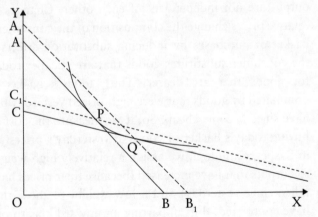

It has sometimes been claimed that the Soviet Union, under Stalin, achieved its astronomical rates of industrial growth in the 1930s, essentially through such statistical legerdemain. Winston Churchill was no doubt alluding to this kind of sleight of hand in his famous description of the three degrees of falsehood: 'lies, damn lies and statistics.'

OPTIMAL ALLOCATION OF TIME

When deciding on their best choices, consumers must take into account not only their income constraint, but their time constraint as well. There are only twenty-four hours in the day and these must be optimally allocated between our various activities. Most notably, we must divide our time between work (which produces money income) and leisure. In this choice, the budget is defined in terms of time (rather than money), the two goods are income and leisure, and the price of leisure relative to income is the wage rate (the amount of money one sacrifices when one opts for one more hour of leisure). The optimal choice is to work up to the point where the MRS of income for leisure just equals the wage rate. If the wage rate rises, this price effect can be decomposed into:

1. An income effect: One is better off at the higher wage and so—if both income and leisure are normal goods—tends to want more income as well as more leisure.
2. A substitution effect: Leisure is now more expensive and so one substitutes more income for it, tending thereby to increase income but reduce leisure.

Both income and substitution effects increase income, which, therefore, necessarily rises when the wage rises; but while the income effect tends to increase leisure, the substitution effect tends to reduce it, so that the net effect is indeterminate. A wage increase may induce people to work more (enjoy less leisure), but it may not necessarily do so. It all depends on the income elasticity of demand for leisure and the substitutability of income for leisure. If everyone else is so busy that one cannot find company to enjoy one's leisure with, people will have little use for additional leisure; and if higher income enables one to buy costly time-saving gadgets, it could easily substitute for more leisure. Higher wages will then induce more work rather than more leisure. On the other hand, if new technologies make leisure-time activities more attractive, if they make reading books or listening to, or playing music easier or accessible to many more, if they facilitate watching movies or picnicking or playing games or adventure sports, they change the indifference map between income and leisure in ways that tend to reduce hours of work.

PROBLEMS

1. If leisure and money income are both normal goods, would a rise in wage rate necessarily induce the individual to work longer hours?
2. If leisure is an inferior good, will this fact affect the impact of a wage rise on hours worked?
3. If good, but expensive, facilities for communicating with distant friends by high-definition videophone become available, how will this affect the responsivcness of labour to wage increase?

Apart from the leisure–labour choice, higher wages also affect the allocation of time between activities with different time requirements. Possibly the most time-consuming of all our standard activities is the bearing and rearing of children. So, as the market penetrates the household, as wages and employment opportunities, particularly of women, increase, female participation in the workforce rises and birth rates fall. Fast food is now the dominant choice when it comes to eating out and T-20 matches draw record crowds while other forms of cricket are played out in empty stadiums. Large families, leisurely restaurant dinners, and Test cricket matches cannot survive the rising price of time. Even as time-honoured a social institution as idle gossip is rapidly being eroded by rising wages—it has virtually vanished from the high-wage Western world and it is endangered even in Asia. Fortunately, the cell phone, by making it possible to gossip while travelling or doing other things, has given this most important cultural activity a new lease of life.

INTERTEMPORAL CONSUMPTION CHOICE

Another type of consumer choice problem refers to the intertemporal allocation of consumption. We have a given stream of income or a given stock of wealth which we must spend over a period, say, over our remaining lifetime. I could choose to save (refrain from consuming) one more rupee today, put it in the bank at an interest rate of 'r' and then get $1 + r$ rupees to consume tomorrow. Whether I do so or not depends on whether I value $1 + r$ rupees of consumption tomorrow more than 1 rupee of current consumption or not. My consumption pattern is optimal when I value the two exactly equally: $1 + r$ rupees of future consumption exactly substitutes for 1 rupee of present consumption. The MRS between consumption in the two periods is equal to the price of consuming in the first period relative to the second, $1 + r$.

How does a rise in interest rate r (and therefore in $1+r$, the price of first-period consumption) affect the levels of consumption and saving? It has:

1. An income effect: The income of savers (who receive higher interest) increases while that of borrowers (who pay higher interest) falls. If consumption is a normal good both today and in the future, these changes tend to increase the consumption of savers in both periods and to reduce that of borrowers in both periods.
2. A substitution effect: The rise in price of present consumption induces both borrowers and savers to save more today and increase consumption tomorrow.

For borrowers, both income and substitution effects tend to reduce present consumption. But for savers, the two effects are opposed. So, while borrowers reduce present consumption when the interest rate rises, we cannot be sure of what savers will do on balance. So, a rise in interest rate may or may not reduce consumption today and increase saving.

An interesting aspect of intertemporal allocation decisions is that they affect the time pattern not only of consumption but also of leisure. The individual's wage rate often varies over his life cycle, implying differences in the opportunity cost of his time in different periods. He then has an incentive to work harder when his earning capacity is at its peak in order to maximize lifetime income. Thus, in a survey of leisure–income choices at a given point of time, high-wage individuals would appear to work more even though, over time, for society as a whole, leisure may increase as wages rise all around.

A similar paradox exists with respect to rates of saving and may have a similar explanation. High-income individuals appear to save a higher proportion of their incomes, yet there seems to be very little correlation between aggregate national savings ratios and per capita incomes. Indeed, much of the highest savings ratios occur in poor countries while very rich nations like the US languish near the bottom of the savings scale. Moreover, in countries where long-run national savings data are available, as in the US, the long-run savings ratio seems largely independent of per capita income. Part of the explanation may lie in the fact that the individual's income varies over his life cycle, inducing him to do more of his lifetime saving in high-income periods, thus generating the cross-sectional relationship between high income and high savings. Of course, other factors must also certainly play a role.

Some economists have argued that the standard indifference curve analysis of consumption and savings decisions is misleading because of the rationality assumption. People often behave irrationally in intertemporal choice. When offered temptations today, they cannot control themselves, even though, at the back of their minds, they know that they will regret this tomorrow. Economists have modelled this behaviour in terms of a game between a consumer's *present self* and his *future selves*. In his cooler moments, the consumer realizes his vulnerability to temptation and his tendency to repent at leisure and so tries to tie the hands of his present self by asking his employer to make deductions (e.g. for provident fund, loan repayments, etc.) from his salary before it is paid to him. But sellers are equally aware of all this and try to offset it by extending consumer credit—through instalment purchase, mortgages and credit cards. Savings behaviour is largely determined by all these institutions.

PROBLEMS

1. Prof. Know All had not been completely chastened by his earlier experience. In his next class, he asserted, 'The interest rate is the price of present consumption

in terms of future consumption. So, as the interest rate rises, present consumption must fall if present consumption is a normal good. If, in some case, present consumption increases as the interest rate rises, present consumption must be a Giffen good.' To his horror, Ms Smarty objected again. Outline her objection this time.

2. Students can buy a travel pass that entitles them to a percentage reduction in the price of all rail tickets.

   a) If a student is indifferent between buying the pass or paying the standard fare, show that he will never spend less and in general will spend more on rail travel if he does buy the pass.

   b) Show that the introduction of such a pass scheme can never reduce the number of rail journeys a student makes.

3. An author receives 15 per cent of the total sales revenue of a book. If he wishes to set a price below that which a publisher favours, it follows that his motive is vanity rather than maximizing his income. Do you agree? (Assume that both the publisher and the author share the same beliefs about demand conditions.)

4. The government wishes to compensate people for the rise in the price of food and is considering two alternative compensation policies:

   a) Selling food at the earlier price while buying it at the current market price, thus absorbing the loss itself.

   b) Giving consumers directly enough money to buy at the new price the amount of food they had earlier been buying. Which of these two alternatives would you advocate? Can you think of a third alternative superior to both?

Chapter 5

The Firm in a Competitive Market

THE NATURE AND OBJECTIVES OF THE FIRM

The market has many advantages over command systems as a means of coordinating the varied activities of an economy. Yet at the heart of the market stands the firm, an institution whose internal structure is entirely hierarchic, a command system par excellence. How do we resolve this paradox? What organizational advantages enable the firm to survive and flourish in the competitive struggle between alternative economic institutions?

The firm is a creature with multiple personalities. It is, in the first place, a production team capable of economies of scale which cannot be achieved through separable individual production processes.[17] In a team, however,

---

[17] Armen Alchian and George Demsetz, 'Production, Information Costs and Economic Organization', *American Economic Review* 62 (1972): 777–95.

the contribution of any individual to output can rarely be isolated or identified. Piece-rate wages, which are based on output, cannot work and must be replaced by time wages. Thus, unless the quality of individual inputs is monitored, moral hazard emerges—the individual is tempted to shirk and free-ride on the efforts of fellow team members. The productivity of teamwork depends on the existence of a monitoring mechanism—work must be monitored and shirking penalized, both of which imply an authority structure within the firm. Further, supervision can be effective only if the reward of the supervisor is linked to his efforts—if he is the full beneficiary of the extra output generated by his efforts. If, in other words, he is the *residual claimant*, the person entitled to claim all that remains after everyone payable by contract has been paid. The modern firm is thus a product of the Industrial Revolution. Earlier, industry was based largely on the *domestic system*. Under this system, the merchant supplied materials to, and collected the finished product from workers who worked at home individually and were paid according to the number of pieces they produced. As the technology of low-cost, large-scale team production evolved, the factory system displaced the domestic. In the factory, time-wage payments supplanted the piece–rate system of domestic production and monitoring of input and disciplinary functions devolved on the profit earner.

The firm is, of course, much more than a production team. It also constitutes an insurance contract that contractually fixes the income of some of its members. It protects them from the risk of market fluctuation while concentrating this risk on the residual claimant. The firm thus offers a variety of roles to potential members, risk-lovers as well as the risk-averse, who achieve, by self-selection, a better sharing of risk than is possible with a uniform payment structure. Insurance, however, creates moral hazard—those whose incomes are contractually fixed have an incentive to shirk, which must be contained by monitoring. Otherwise, bankruptcy for the insurer (the residual claimant) is assured. Insurance, therefore, cannot be provided by an external agency; it must be supplied from within the production process by the monitor himself.

The firm also represents an incompletely specified contract—in an uncertain world, a detailed specification of what an employee might be required to do in each of the thousands of possible contingencies would be prohibitively costly. If the firm is to keep such transaction costs within manageable limits while retaining flexibility and adaptability to changing circumstances, the employee must, within certain broad limits, undertake to do as he is told by his authorized superiors. It is this contractual surrender of discretion by some people to others that is the basis of hierarchy. The firm is thus a command structure but one that is generated by contract.

Finally, the firm is a safeguard against opportunism:[18] some firms evolve due to the cost, not of writing but of enforcing contracts. A long-run relationship where one partner has invested in assets specific to that relationship tempts the other partner to hold out on the first. The owner of the specific assets is vulnerable to blackmail, given the cost of enforcing his contracts with others. A steel-maker who builds furnaces designed for a particular quality of

---

[18] Oliver Williamson, *Markets and Hierarchies: Analysis and Antitrust Implications* (New York: The Free Press, 1975).

coal is at the mercy of the mine-owner who controls the supply of coal of this variety. The problem disappears if the partners are members of the same firm and are linked by its formal authority structure.

WHY ARE CAPITALISTS BOSSES?

All this implies that there should be a residual claimant who bears the major risks faced by the firm and that the supervisory, disciplinary and decision-making functions of the firm should vest in him. It does not necessarily imply that the capitalist—the owner and supplier of capital— should be the residual claimant and the boss. Indeed, the typical medieval firm under the guild system was owned, not by capitalists but by workers—it used borrowed capital, for which it paid a contractually fixed price, and reserved the variable residue (after capital and other costs had been paid) for the workers.

The rise of the modern capitalist firm was associated with an increase in the capitalist's ability and willingness to bear risk. Unlike labour, capital is a highly divisible resource; the growth of the share market enabled capitalists to divide their resources among many uncorrelated industries, thus reducing the possible variance of returns by diversification. The share market made the capitalist essentially neutral to the risks of a particular business. The worker could not diversify his allocation of labour between industries to a similar extent. The fixed length of the working day as well as the limited human capacity to learn confined him to one, or a few jobs. Unlike the capitalist, the worker remained risk-averse. Optimally therefore, risk could be concentrated on the capitalist; he became the residual claimant and therefore the boss.

The growth of the share market was stimulated by the principle of limited liability. By restricting the liability of the investor for the losses of a business to his personal stake in it, the principle encouraged equity investment— participation in the fortunes of a business as a shareholder. It also discouraged lending to the firm. In the event of loss, the owner was responsible for repaying the loans taken by the firm, not fully, but only to the extent of his own stake in it. This generated moral hazard: the owner was tempted into imprudent risk-taking with borrowed capital. Thus, limited liability in a worker-owned firm created incentives for wasteful and speculative use of capital which, in turn, deterred potential investors. The owner had to be the major source of funds himself since he alone could supervise their end use. The capitalist became the owner and therefore the boss.

LARGE-SCALE PRODUCTION AND THE INSTITUTIONAL STRUCTURE OF THE FIRM

The factory system, the wage system, the share market, the principle of limited liability and the firm, especially the capitalist firm, are thus inextricably interlinked. Central to this complex of institutions was the evolution of large-scale technology. Large-scale production did more than foster factories, time wages and teamwork with supervisory hierarchies. Its heavy fixed-capital requirements involved far too much risk for the individual owner to finance or underwrite: it necessitated the pooling of risk and therefore the rise of the share market. Fixed assets are also generally specific to particular uses; firms dependent on them require increased flexibility in labour use if they are to adapt to changing circumstances. This, in turn, reinforces the need for an agreed surrender of discretion by labour and a strong structure of authority. Finally, asset specificity increases the scope for opportunistic exploitation of the firm by those with whom the fixed commitment constitutes a long-term link; it makes it necessary for the firm to expand so as to make these outsiders part of itself.

THE STANDARD THEORY OF THE FIRM

Despite the fact that the firm is not a simple profit-maximizer but a complex institution with many agency problems, we picture it, in elementary economics, for the sake of simplicity, as a unitary organization that aims at profit maximization.

In this picture, the firm makes two key decisions: it chooses the scale of production and the technique of production. We consider these two decisions in the reverse order.

Choice of technique implies deciding on the combination of factors that minimizes the cost of producing any given output. This is best understood in terms of an *isoquant map*, which is a picture of the production technology of any product. An isoquant is a curve connecting all the combinations of labour and capital that generate a given output (hence the term isoquant, i.e. equal quantities) rather like an indifference curve that connects all the combinations of goods X and Y that yield the same level of satisfaction. The isoquant map is the entire set of isoquants for a given product. The properties of the typical isoquant are similar to those of the typical indifference curve: it slopes downward to the right, implying substitutability between factors. However, as with goods, substitutability between factors is never perfect (if it were, the factors would be identical given the appropriate choice of units). So, as the input of factor Y diminishes, more and more of factor X is needed to replace successive units of Y. The marginal rate of factor substitution (the slope of the isoquant) diminishes, so that the isoquant, like the indifference curve, is convex to the origin. As with indifference curves and satisfaction levels, higher isoquants represent higher levels of output.

Fig. 5.1: Isoquants and Isocost Lines

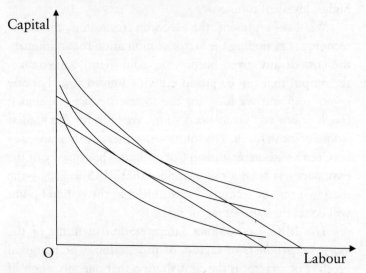

On the isoquant map, we superimpose a set of *isocost lines* (Fig. 5.1). An isocost line connects the set of factors that cost the firm a fixed amount. It is like a budget line that connects different baskets of goods that cost the same. It slopes down to the right. The slope is the additional amount of factor X (capital in Fig. 5.1). I could buy with the money I save by buying one unit less Y (labour in

Fig. 5.1). By reducing my purchases of labour by one unit, I save the wage p_L I would have paid for it. With the amount of money p_L, I can buy p_L/p_K units of capital (where p_K is the price of the services of capital). Thus the slope of the isocost line is the ratio of factor prices. If the firm is too small to influence the prices of factors of production and must take them as given parameters, this slope (which is equal to the ratio of the factor prices) will be constant—so that the isocost line is linear. Higher isocost lines represent higher levels of total cost.

We can represent the decision regarding choice of techniques as finding the factor combination that minimizes the cost of any given output, or, equivalently, maximizes the output that can be produced with a given cost. For any given isoquant, we look for the lowest isocost line that it touches. For any given isocost line, we look for the highest isoquant it can reach. The solution in either case is a tangency between an isoquant and an isocost line. The equality of the two slopes at such a point implies that MRS = p_L/p_K —the marginal rate of technical substitution at the optimal point will equal the ratio of factor prices.

The MRS has another interpretation in terms of the *marginal products* of factors of production. The marginal product of a factor is the contribution that one more unit of a factor would make to output. If I reduce labour input by one unit, my output diminishes by MP_L. To compensate for this so that I can stay on the same isoquant, I need MP_L/MP_K units of capital. The MRS is also the ratio of the marginal products of the factors of production. Thus, at the cost minimizing technique, $MP_L/MP_K = p_L/p_K$.

A higher isoquant can be tangential only to a higher isocost line: as output increases, so does the minimized total cost of production. There is a whole family of such tangencies, each for a separate scale of output. The curve connecting these points of tangency is known as the *expansion path* of the firm and shows how its input pattern changes as its scale of production expands.

Figure 5.2: Homothetic Isoquants

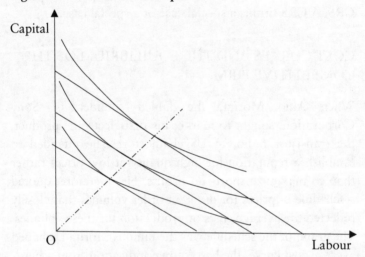

A special kind of isoquant map is one where the expansion paths are all rays through the origin (Fig. 5.2). This would happen if the isoquants are all parallel along such rays—they are radially parallel. Such an isoquant map is called *homothetic*. With homothetic isoquants, the optimal ratio of capital to labour will be independent of the scale of output; it will depend only on the price ratio of factors of production p_L/p_K. Along any ray through the origin (which, for homothetic isoquants, coincides with an expansion path), the two inputs increase in the same proportion. If, further, the output also increases in the same proportion, we have what is called *constant returns to scale* (CRS). Along the expansion path of a CRS firm, the productivities of the factors are constant since output increases in proportion to the two inputs.

Note, however, that not all isoquant maps are homothetic and that not all homothetic isoquant maps are CRS. A CRS firm is a special case of a special case.

COST CURVES AND THE EQUILIBRIUM OF THE COMPETITIVE FIRM

When Akio Morita, the fabled founder of Sony Corporation, sought to market his first electronic product, the transistor radio, to US chain stores, he intended to establish a reputation for high quality at low prices rather than to maximize short-run profits. He, therefore, quoted a schedule of prices for different order volumes that closely reflected the average costs of production for these volumes. The graph of the schedule was the famous Morita U-shaped average cost curve, the best-known indication from a hard-headed businessman that economic theorizing on this issue was not entirely fanciful.

How did Morita derive his average cost curve? Behind his calculations lay decisions about optimal technique, about the cheapest way of producing any given output. As the firm increased output along its expansion path, the minimum cost of producing this output increased, generating a *total cost curve*. The slope of this curve was the *marginal cost* (MC), the additional cost of producing one more unit of output. The marginal cost curve, relating marginal cost to output, could be derived from the total cost curve. So could the curve of average cost (AC), the ratio of total cost to output.

For CRS technologies, AC is independent of output; so is MC, which in this case is equal to AC. The AC and MC curves are horizontal and in fact coincide. For increasing returns to scale (IRS), AC and MC drop as scale expands, so that the AC and MC curves are downward sloping. Diminishing returns to scale (DRS), on the other hand, imply rising AC and MC curves. I shall explain shortly how IRS and DRS may arise.

The AC curve of the typical firm is U-shaped. An initial IRS phase is followed by DRS: AC is minimum at the point of transition. The MC curve is also U-shaped. MC is below AC when AC is falling and above AC when AC is rising (MC pulls down AC when MC is lower, and pulls it up when higher). At the minimum point of the AC curve, MC = AC (see Fig. 5.3).

The Average–Margin Relationship

The relationship between the average and the margin—between price (P) and marginal revenue (MR)[19] or between average cost (AC) and marginal cost (MC)—is best understood by cricket fans (who constitute the vast majority of the Indian population) in terms of the relationship between runs per over (the average) and the runs made in the last over (the margin). If the runs made in the last over exceeded the average run rate, the

[19] Marginal revenue is the addition to total revenue due to a unit increase in output sold.

latter would rise; if it fell short, the run rate would fall. The average falls when the margin is less than it and rises when the margin is more; it is stationary when the average and the margin are equal.

A slightly more formal account of the relationship (say, between P and MR) is as follows: As P falls, it is not only the price of the last unit that has fallen but that of all the earlier units as well. Thus, total revenue increases by less than P: MR < P. The difference is the product of two factors: (1) total sales volume, and (2) the fall in P due to the last unit increase in sales.

$$P - MR = Q \cdot \Delta P / \Delta Q$$

where Q represents total sales volume, ΔQ is a marginal increase in sales and ΔP, the marginal fall in price that it induces. The second of these factors is nothing but the downward slope of the demand curve. So if, at any sales volume Q, we know the price P and the slope of the demand curve, we also know the MR. The marginal value is uniquely determined by the average value and the slope of the average curve at this point.

Precisely the same relationship holds between AC and MC, and indeed between any average and the corresponding marginal variable.

If, therefore, a demand curve and an AC curve are tangential at some output (i.e. they share the same average value and the same slope), the corresponding marginal values will also match: MR = MC at this output. This is a result that we shall use in later chapters.

Fig. 5.3: Firm's Average and Marginal Cost Curves

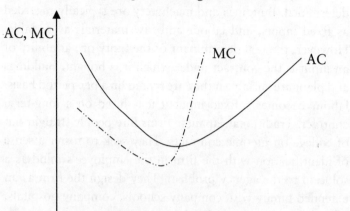

Note that the costs of the firm include an allowance for the entrepreneur just enough to prevent him from leaving the industry, a *normal profit* equivalent to what he could earn in other industries.

IRS is usually the result of a fixed input or mode of organization which comes in minimum indivisible units. Examples: a machine that will not work or is not available below a minimum size, a division of labour that requires one specialist for each different operation. As the firm expands, this fixed cost is spread over a larger output, so that unit cost declines.

DRS also has a similar source—as output increases, the fixed plant and buildings get overcrowded, and the capacity of each specialist is strained, so that beyond a point efficiency declines and unit cost rises. What happens here is that unit *variable* cost rises fast enough to offset the falling unit fixed costs.

We tend to think of fixed inputs and cost as technologically determined. Buildings and machinery are typically regarded as fixed inputs, and labour and raw materials as variable. However, the real determinant of the fixity or variability of an input is the contract under which it is bought. Buildings and plant are variable if they are rented on a per-period basis; labour becomes a fixed input if it is hired on a long-term contract. Traditional Japanese firms hire people straight out of college on lifetime contracts. They seek to foster a sense of identification with the firm in the employee's mind as a solution to the agency problem. They design the firm as an extended family with company schools, company hospitals, company vacations and drinking parties, company sports and company lunches. No one is dismissed even in severe recessions or for any reason other than major misconduct. In consequence, labour becomes a fixed factor.

All contracts, however, have a limited duration. If we consider a period long enough for contracts to lapse or for equipment, etc. that has been bought (rather than rented) to wear out, all these costs become variable. Thus, while there may be many fixed costs in the short run, there are hardly any in the long run. A distinction needs to be made between short-run and long-run costs.

In the long run, even though there may be no fixed factors, some indivisibilities may exist. For example, one cannot have less than one specialist worker. Therefore, a division of labour requires a minimum workforce and a minimum scale of production below which it is underutilized. Thus, there may be IRS at small scales of production in the long run, despite the absence of fixed factors.

What about the shape of the long-run average cost (LAC) curve at large scales of production? Once IRS is exhausted, we reach minimum LAC. Can we not replicate the mode of production we have reached and expand output indefinitely at this minimum average cost? Unfortunately not. As production multiplies, so do problems of coordination. Coordination, by its very nature, is a unitary function—if we try to delegate the function to a number of coordinators, the problem arises of coordinating the coordinators. Coordination, in short, is a fixed factor even in the long run. Consequently, as output expands, the increase in problems to be solved and decisions to be made strains the limited capacity of the coordinator and leads to rising LAC. Thus, even the LAC curve is U-shaped.

PROBLEM

1. At Sita's pizza shop, it costs Rs 5000 to make 100 pizzas. When 101 pizzas are made, total costs rise to Rs 5060. Then we can conclude that:
    a) Total fixed costs are falling.
    b) Marginal costs are falling.
    c) Average costs are falling.
    d) Average costs are rising.

Given his cost curves, how does the producer choose his scale of output? If he believes he is too small to affect prices and must take the market price as a parameter (perfect competition), the best output for him to produce is that at which marginal cost equals price (when we are on the rising segment of the MC curve). At smaller outputs, MC < P, the cost of producing another unit is less than the revenue it will earn, so that another unit adds to profits. At larger outputs, P < MC, the last unit earned is less than its cost, so that it is profitable to reduce production. Only when P = MC is there no incentive to change output at the margin. However, the producer also has the option of shutting down altogether. He will exercise this option if this minimizes his losses. In the short run, he has fixed costs which he continues to incur even if he ceases production (see Fig. 5.4).

Why do we add the rider that the producer should be on the rising segment of his MC curve? If P = MC when MC is falling, the producer is minimizing, not maximizing, his profit. If he produced one more unit, MC would fall below P, implying that the additional unit adds to his profits. If he produced one unit less, MC would rise above P, implying that the costs he saves by contracting output exceed the sales revenue he loses, so that he is again adding to his profits. Deviations in either direction from his current output level are profitable—he is currently doing the worst possible thing for himself, not the best.

Fig. 5.4: Firm's Short-Run Cost Curves

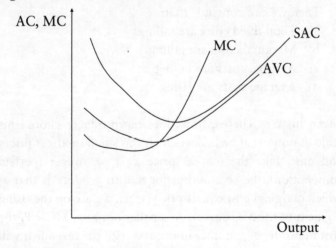

As long as the price covers the producer's variable cost, it is worth his while to continue producing. His shutdown price is

P = AVC at the minimum point of the AVC curve. Below the minimum AVC, he is not even recouping his variable costs, so that he will add to his losses if he continues producing. Thus, the conditions for the short-run equilibrium of the firm are (1) P = MC, (2) MC is increasing, (3) P ≥ AVC (see Fig. 5.5).

PROBLEMS

1. Prof. Know All was lecturing his economics class: 'In times of depression, firms with permanent workers survive while firms manned by temporary labour fold up. This shows that permanent labour is more efficient than temporary.' Ms Smarty, as usual, dissented. What do you think it was this time?

2. Japan has often been accused of 'dumping': selling abroad at prices below AC in order to capture foreign markets. Can you think of an alternative explanation of Japan's very low prices?

Fig. 5.5: Firm in Short-Run Equilibrium

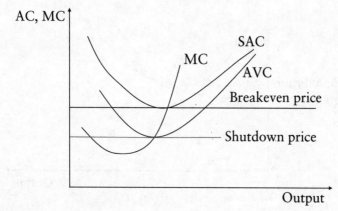

In the long run, there are no fixed costs and consequently entry and exit of firms in and out of the industry is free. Since all costs are variable, price must in equilibrium equal the average of all long-run costs; P = LAC. If P falls short of LAC, profits will be subnormal—the firm will be earning less than it could in other industries and so will migrate elsewhere. The decline in number of firms leads to a contraction in output and a consequent rise in P. Further, if P exceeds LAC, the firm will be making excess profits, higher than what can be earned elsewhere. This attracts other firms into the industry and a consequent expansion of industry output, which drives down P. Thus, in long-run equilibrium, P will converge on LAC. Further, since profit maximization requires P = MC, the equilibrium condition becomes P = LMC = LAC, which is possible only at the minimum point of the LAC curve. In long-run equilibrium, there will be no excess profits (see Fig. 5.6).

Fig. 5.6: Firm in Long-Run Equilibrium

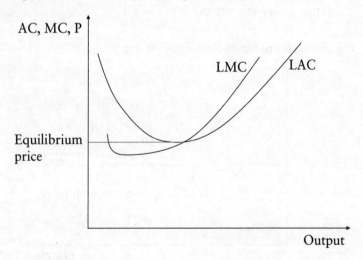

It is the comparison of P and LAC that dictates the firm's choice of product. The firm migrates away from industries where P < LAC to those where P > LAC. This is the process that ensures the long-run equilibrium of the industry.

Profit maximization by the firm has implications for the intensity with which factors are used. Since an additional unit of labour adds an amount MP_L to output, an additional unit of output requires an amount $1/MP_L$ of labour, which costs p_l/MP_L. Thus, $MC = p_L/MP_L$. Since $MC = P$ for profit maximization, we infer that $P . MP_L = p_L$. The firm equates the value of the marginal product of a factor to its price. This implies that factors are paid according to their contribution to the product (after allowing for the contribution of other factors as well).

THE SUPPLY CURVE OF THE COMPETITIVE INDUSTRY

From the reaction of the firm to market prices, we can figure out the supply curve of the industry. In the short run, the number of firms in the industry is fixed—so the industry supply curve is simply the horizontal sum of what might be called the individual supply curve of each firm. From the conditions for short-run equilibrium, the latter is the rising segment of the firm's MC curve above the minimum point of the AVC curve. Below minimum AVC, supply is zero.

In the long run, however, the number of firms is also variable, so the industry supply curve cannot be derived by simply summing the supply curves of individual firms. Further, we need to consider the impact of new entry on the cost curves of the firms. If all firms, incumbents as well as new entrants, have access to the same technology and resources, their cost curves will be identical. Then, if there are no externalities, positive or negative, the industry could expand through the multiplication of identical firms, all producing at their identical minimum LAC. The long-run supply curve of the industry is horizontal at the level of this minimum LAC. Things are different if there are externalities.

1. Negative externalities: If there is a limited supply of the resources required by the industry, its expansion will drive up the prices of these resources and the cost curves of all firms in the industry. The minimum LAC point will also rise, so that a larger supply will be associated with a higher price. The industry supply curve will be upward sloping.

2. Positive externalities: If the growth of the industry results in internal economies of scale in its supplier industries, this will cheapen the inputs supplied by the latter. For example, the growth of industry results in larger demand for electricity which can support larger power plants generating cheaper electricity, or a better developed road or rail network supplying cheaper transportation. If this effect dominates, the cost curves of all firms will be lowered by it: the industry supply curve will slope downwards, unlike the usual picture of a supply curve. Such a supply curve, as already noted, may lead to an unstable market.

PROBLEM

1. As oil output rose, oil prices increased, but as computer output increased, computer prices fell. Why?

RISING AND FALLING SUPPLY CURVES IN WAR
AND INDUSTRIALIZATION

Two well-known historical examples illustrate the important
consequences of long-run supply curves of different shapes:

1. The world's largest marine ecosystem lies off the coasts
   of Peru and Chile. These coasts are washed by the cool
   Humboldt current which displaces warmer surface
   waters, producing an upwelling of cold water from the
   ocean depths rich in plankton and other microorganisms.
   This attracts vast shoals of anchovy, krill, sardines and
   other sea fish, which, in turn, act as irresistible magnets
   for pelicans, gulls, cormorants and other seabirds. The
   birds gorge themselves on the fish and defecate, so
   that every evening hundreds of tons of potassium- and
   phosphorus-rich manure descend like manna from heaven
   on the shores of the Atacama desert and the adjacent
   islands. The resulting guano deposits constitute the
   world's best organic fertilizer. Like all natural resources,
   however, the supply is not augmentable at will. Now,
   the enormous expansion of agriculture in the second half
   of the nineteenth century generated a booming demand
   for fertilizers. Since effective chemical fertilizers were not
   invented till the early twentieth century, the demand for
   guano soared. As its price skyrocketed, so did the value
   of the uninhabited Atacama desert, so much so indeed
   that between 1879 and 1883, a bloody full-scale war
   between Chile, Bolivia and Peru erupted over its control.
   The War of the Pacific is the only war in recorded history
   fought over a pile of bird dung.
2. As western Europe industrialized in the nineteenth
   century, the rapid growth of agricultural exports from

the New World to feed Europe was associated with economies of scale in transportation—the extension of the railway network, the installation of elevators and silos for the bulk handling of grain, and the induction of steam-propelled ocean freighters and refrigerator ships that spectacularly reduced the delivery price of food in Europe. The importance of this in averting the Malthusian–Ricardian crisis that threatened European industrialization earlier in the century and indeed in defusing the proletarian revolution that Marx and his followers had been eagerly predicting since 1848 can hardly be overestimated.

THE OPTIMALITY OF COMPETITIVE EQUILIBRIUM

We have discussed the existence and stability of competitive equilibrium, thus seeing how the competitive market conjures up order out of potential chaos. The question remains of its *optimality*—is this a just or desirable order? The issue of justice lies essentially outside the realm of economics; it is an ethical issue. However, if we believe that the value of any form of social organization is related to the satisfaction of the individuals in the relevant society, we can agree on a minimalist criterion of optimality. Our social arrangements should not leave unexploited any opportunity to make one person better off without hurting anyone else. This is the Pareto-criterion.[20] A Pareto-optimum is a situation in which it is impossible to make anyone better off without making someone else worse off.

---

[20] Vilfredo Pareto, *Manual of Political Economy*, trans. Ann S. Schwier (New York: Augustus M. Kelley Publishers, 1971).

The first theorem of welfare economics tells us that any competitive equilibrium is Pareto-optimal. Consider first a *prisoner-of-war* economy (a pure exchange economy in which there is no production). If a competitive market establishes itself here, every individual equates his MRS between any pair of goods (say, X and Y) to the market-price ratio in equilibrium. Since this is a common factor, all individuals will have the same MRS (say, the number m). Now, if we are to redistribute goods so as to make individual I better off, we must give him one unit more of X (say) while taking away less than m units of Y. This unit of X must come from someone else, say, individual II. Can individual II be compensated? Not if we can only spare less than an additional m units of Y for this purpose, because his MRS is also m in equilibrium. He would need m units of Y to offset the loss of a unit of X. Thus, in competitive equilibrium, no such Pareto-improvements are possible. We are at a Pareto-optimum.

The same proposition holds when we introduce production into the picture, provided there is full employment of resources. The new question that arises here is whether the composition of the output basket can be changed in a way that makes someone better off without hurting anyone else. If all resources are fully employed, one can increase a particular output (say, X) only by diverting a factor (say, labour) into its production from some other output (say, Y) that it was producing. If we transfer one unit of labour from the production of Y to X, we sacrifice an amount MP_{LY} of Y for MP_{LX} of X; we are transforming Y into X at the marginal rate MP_{LY}/MP_{LX}. Recall that in a competitive equilibrium, the price of labour is equal to the value of its marginal product in terms of any output. So,

$MP_{LY}/MP_{LX} = p_L/P_Y \div p_L/P_X = P_X/P_Y$. But the price ratio of X to Y is also every consumer's MRS between the two goods. Suppose that the common marginal rate of transformation or MRT (which is equal in equilibrium to the MRS) is t. Consider whether we can improve the lot of individual I in this equilibrium by changing the output mix. If we give him one more unit of X, he will be better off if he has to sacrifice less than t units of Y (since his MRS is t). But the technology is not productive enough to transform less than t units of Y into one unit of X. Therefore, if individual I is to be made better off, we must find some more Y to transform into X; this Y must be taken away from some other individual, thus making the latter worse off. Thus, a Pareto-improvement is impossible in this case either; we are at a Pareto-optimum.

The first theorem of welfare economics does not imply that the competitive allocation of goods is socially desirable in any sense other than that of efficiency (the avoidance of waste). For instance, an allocation of all goods to one person, leaving all others with nothing, is Pareto-optimal but not very desirable. Fortunately, there is also a second theorem (developed by Kenneth Arrow) that says that any desired allocation of goods can be achieved efficiently if we redistribute the initial assets of everyone by appropriate lump-sum transfers and then let them trade among themselves in a competitive market. Of course, such lump-sum transfers are very difficult to accomplish.

PROBLEMS

1. Jack Sprat could eat no fat,
    His wife could eat no lean,
    And so between them both you see,

They licked the platter clean.

How many Pareto-optimal allocations are there in the Sprat household?

2. Fatty, Smarty and the rest of their family are sharing Fatty's birthday cake. Consider each of the following possible scenarios:

   a) They all get equal shares.

   b) Fatty grabs the whole cake and gobbles it up.

   c) Mother tells Fatty that he must not be greedy and should leave something for the others. Fatty says that if he isn't going to get the whole cake, he would prefer that nobody gets anything. He then grabs the cake, throws it on the ground and stamps on it.

   d) While the family is debating the sharing arrangements, a monkey (definitely not a member of the family) seizes a part of the cake and makes off.

All the while, Smarty, who has an economics test coming up, has been figuring out which of these allocations are Pareto-optimal and which are not. What do you think are her conclusions?

Chapter 6

Monopoly

The competitive firm conforms to the basic requirements of an orderly equilibrium. It is a price-taker: it adapts to the price ruling in the market and lacks the power to manipulate this. It faces a demand curve that is horizontal, perfectly elastic at the prevailing price even though the demand curve for the industry as a whole is downward sloping. In imperfect competition, however, each individual firm faces a down-sloping demand curve for its product. It is a *price-maker* whose output decisions affect the market price. As we have argued, in such circumstances, the informational value of price signals gets blurred.

What are the sources of imperfections of competition and to what extent do they disrupt the equilibrating and optimizing functions of the market? Typically, an industry with only a small number of firms can be expected to be imperfectly competitive. We examine the polar case where there is only one firm in the industry, the case generally described as monopoly.

A monopolist is the sole seller of a good with no close substitutes. Such a situation cannot be sustained for long unless rivals are somehow deterred from entering the industry. How are such entry barriers created?

The most obvious kind of entry barrier is the exclusive ownership of a specific resource indispensable for the industry. The ownership of the diamond belts of South Africa, Botswana and Namibia is the basis of the De Beers monopoly of the raw diamond business. During the eighteenth and most of the nineteenth century, Brazil enjoyed a monopoly of natural rubber production because the rubber plant was unknown outside the Amazon basin. However, while diamonds were minerals with a distribution strictly determined by geology, natural rubber was a vegetable product and could be readily transplanted in other equatorial climates. Towards the end of the nineteenth century, the British explorer Henry Wickham, 'the thief at the end of the world', famously 'stole' 70,000 rubber seeds from Amazonia and smuggled them to the Royal Botanical Gardens at Kew. Rubber seedlings from Kew transplanted in Malaysia, Indonesia and Sri Lanka produced the deluge of natural rubber that broke the Brazilian monopoly just at the time when bicycle and automobile tyres, industrial gaskets and rubber-coated electric and telegraph wires were setting off a worldwide explosion in demand for rubber.

A second species of entry barriers are those erected by government through licensing policy or patents. During the mercantilist age deplored by Adam Smith, government bestrode the economy like a colossus, dictating who should produce what—sometimes indeed how and how much as well. Licences enmeshed all industry, acting as lucrative sources of income, formally for the government as it sold charters of monopoly, and less formally for the licensing officials who dispensed licences in exchange for bribes. The various East India Companies, the English, the French, the Dutch, all functioned under charters of monopoly bought from their respective governments. In India, before the reforms of 1991, many industries were transformed into effective monopolies by licensing policy.

Patents constitute a different kind of legal entry barrier. As is well known, the research to generate new knowledge is expensive and uncertain of bearing fruit, but the replication of an already-developed technology is easy and cheap. Without the establishment of property rights in new knowledge, innovation would have been a hazardous and profitless business and technological progress nearly impossible. The patent is a device designed to protect the incentive to innovate by granting the inventor the exclusive right to use the knowledge he has created for a limited period. For this period, however, the patent is a charter of monopoly.

An entry barrier created neither by geography nor by government but by the interaction of technology and market size is the *natural monopoly*. This emerges when one firm can supply the market more efficiently than two, so that the incumbent can sell at prices that cannot possibly be matched by a new entrant. Natural monopolies are based on economies of scale that are substantial in relation to market size. Therefore, as the market expands, a natural monopoly may well be disrupted by the entry of new competitors. Railways, with their vast economies of scale at every level, represent a classic example of a natural monopoly. Other examples are more difficult to produce since whether an industry is a natural monopoly or not depends not only on its technology but also on the size of the market in which it operates. One aspect of economies of scale—which is linked not to reductions in unit cost but to increase in the attractiveness of the product to new users—is *network externality*. As a telephone network expands, it can offer lower rates for calls within the system. The larger the network, the higher the probability that my calls will be internal to the system and will therefore cost less, the more attractive therefore is the network itself. Network externalities exist in railway systems as well, but in telecommunications, they are a paramount consideration.

Railways also exemplify another kind of entry barrier—large sunk cost. It is a cost that, once incurred, is irrecoverable. High sunk cost implies a high degree of risk, discouraging entrants directly and reducing their access to credit and share capital. Also, high sunk costs are generally associated with relatively low variable costs, so that the incumbent's implicit threat of retaliation against new entry becomes credible.

A final issue, related to network externality but unfamiliar enough to deserve a fuller explanation, is that of credibility. Consider an auditor hired by a firm to certify its financial soundness for the information of its investors. The auditor is constantly tempted to collude with the firm for a consideration and to conceal its misdeeds. However, if collusion is detected in a single instance, the credibility of the auditor—and therefore his usefulness to investors—melts away. Now the probability of detection of collusion increases with the number of collusions, which in turn increases with the number of the auditor's clients. Thus, an auditor with a large clientele has a stronger incentive to stay honest than one with very few clients and is therefore more attractive to investors. Similarly, an airline with a large network of flights runs a larger risk of a disastrous

accident that could destroy its reputation and is therefore
more likely to take safety precautions than a smaller airline.
In both cases, the consumer's faith in the larger firm may
pose an insuperable barrier to the entry of new rivals.

THE PROFIT-MAXIMIZING MONOPOLIST

Unlike the horizontal demand curve of the perfect competitor,
the monopolist's demand curve slopes downward. He has
no rivals whose markets he can invade without reducing his
own price significantly. If he is to sell more, he must cut
his price. However, his marginal revenue—the increase in
revenue achieved by selling one more unit—is less than his
price (because he must reduce price not only on the last unit
sold but on all the infra-marginal units as well). The MR
curve, therefore, must lie below the demand curve and, like
it, slope down as well (Fig. 6.1).

Profit maximization requires the marginal cost curve to
cut the MR curve from below. At scales of output lower
than this intersection, MR > MC, the monopolist adds to his
profits by expanding production. At larger scales, MC > MR,
so that contraction is profitable. Thus, the monopolist
maximizes his profit by equating MC to MR.

Since P > MR, it follows that, in monopoly equilibrium,
P > MC. The gap between P and MR, and therefore between P
and MC, is inversely related to the price-elasticity of demand.
If the elasticity is infinite, the demand curve is horizontal and
P = MR = MC; we are in a competitive equilibrium. There
is no gap between price and marginal cost, and production
is optimal. This represents the case where the seller can sell
any amount he wishes at the ruling price. This implies that
he does not have to reduce the price of infra-marginal units

when he expands production. Therefore, MR = P. On the other hand, if elasticity is less than 1, demand will rise less than proportionately to any fall in price. Recalling Chapter 4, the total consumer expenditure (and therefore sales revenue) will fall: MR will be negative. If elasticity is equal to 1, the rise in demand is proportional to the fall in price, and sales revenue is independent of output so that MR = 0. Thus, if MC is positive, MR = MC can only be achieved where the elasticity of demand is more than 1. Monopoly equilibrium is possible only on the elastic segment of the demand curve.

Unlike the competitive firm, the monopolist has no supply curve. There is no functional relationship between output and the price required to induce it. At any output, the price that the monopolist will charge depends on the elasticity of demand, as explained in the previous paragraph. Different demand conditions will give rise to different supply prices for the same output.

Fig. 6.1: Profit Maximization by a Monopolist

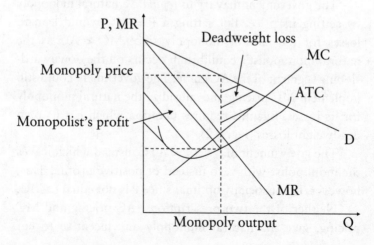

MONOPOLY AND PUBLIC POLICY

A monopoly equilibrium with P > MC implies that some people who value the good more than its MC but less than the price that the monopolist has set for it, cannot participate in the market. Socially, this is a suboptimal situation. Monopoly has resulted in restriction of output below the optimal level, creating a *deadweight loss*. Can public policy improve the situation?

The government may use antitrust laws to break up large companies or prevent mergers between them. The US government used the Sherman Antitrust Act in 1911 to break up the American Tobacco Company and Rockefeller's Standard Oil Company of New Jersey and in 1982 to break up American Telephone and Telegraph. But mergers could have benefits associated with joint production. The government has to weigh these benefits against the costs of reduced competition due to the merger.

The government may try to *regulate* a natural monopoly by setting its price. But setting a P = MC would lead to losses for the natural monopoly since MC < AC as the natural monopolist's equilibrium occurs on the downward-sloping segment of the AC curve. The government could still implement MC pricing and subsidize the natural monopoly for its losses. But this requires taxation which has its own deadweight losses (Fig. 6.2).

The government may set P = ATC instead which leaves the monopolist with zero instead of positive profits. This, however, is not socially optimal since P is not equal to MC.

Neither of the two prescriptions, AC pricing and MC pricing, give the natural monopoly any incentive to cut costs, since price will always be adjusted to cover costs. Another alternative is the public ownership of monopolies like utility companies. But this again injures cost-cutting incentives.

The costs associated with imperfect policies may be greater than the welfare costs of monopoly.

Fig. 6.2: Marginal-Cost Pricing in a Natural Monopoly

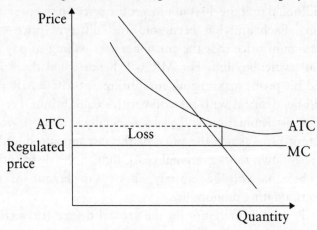

The essence of monopoly power is the ability to exclude rival producers from a particular market. An even larger degree of power is represented by the ability to divide up the market into separable sub-markets between which no *arbitrage* is possible: no one, other than the monopolist himself, can buy in the cheaper sub-market to sell dear. A monopolist armed with this weapon can increase his profits even further by charging different prices in each sub-market. There are three species of such *price discrimination*.

Perfect or first-degree price discrimination involves a customized all-or-nothing offer to each consumer based on his willingness to pay for any given quantity so as to extract his entire consumer surplus. The seller cannot implement this without the knowledge of the customer's demand curve, though he may, of course, try to discover this by bargaining. If he is successful, his revenue will be the entire area under the demand curve. When he sells an additional unit, he does not lower the price on the previous units. Each unit has been sold at a different price—the maximum price that the consumer was willing to pay for that particular unit. His MR will hence equal the price, and his profit maximizing equilibrium, at MC = MR = P, will be identical with the competitive equilibrium. Perfect price discrimination will yield a socially optimal level of output price (since the price of the last unit produced is driven down to its marginal cost), though the distribution of benefits will be entirely skewed in favour of the discriminating monopolist.

Price discrimination in the second degree (or vertical price discrimination) is less exacting for the seller in terms of its information requirements. It involves quantity discounts for bulk orders and requires the producer to know his own technology (as in the example given earlier of the Morita cost curve) rather than anything related to the customer.

Third-degree price discrimination differentiates consumers on the basis of observable characteristics or behaviour. It involves discounts to more price-conscious groups of customers such as students or the elderly and higher prices for others. It means higher prices for ice cream at the beach or the zoo and for beverages and water at high-end restaurants where people go to splurge rather than to pinch pennies. It implies discounts for price-sensitive customers who take the time and trouble to clip coupons out of newspapers. Sometimes third-degree discrimination overlaps with second degree—minor improvements in quality are described by the seller as designed for the elite and sold at astronomical prices to those who want to distinguish themselves as the creme de la crème. Such also, in large measure, is the secret of branded products.

The discriminating monopolist who supplies several markets from a common production facility maximizes profit by equating the MR in each market to the common MC, and therefore to each other. Further, since the gap between MR and price is inversely related to the elasticity of demand, he will charge higher prices in the less elastic market. This has an important bearing in international trade. Where international markets are effectively separated, a monopoly producer will set lower prices in poorer countries where demand is likely to be highly sensitive to price.

Separability of markets is crucial to price discrimination. In practice, however, the walls between markets are typically porous. Thus, the price differential between the ice cream at the beach and in the bazaar will be eroded by new entry at the beach down to the transport cost of ice cream between the two sites. Excess profits, if any, will be entirely due to transport advantages. High-end restaurants must first establish a reputational monopoly, perhaps through expensive decor or high-priced chefs, before they can charge extortionate prices for tea and water. One cannot bar one's rivals from also offering discounts to coupon-clippers or the elderly or students, thereby driving excess profits from exploiting each segment of the market down to zero. Only if there are real barriers to entry into the particular sub-markets that one firm controls and fleeces will price discrimination yield excess profits. It may happen, but the price differentials will reflect real differences in unit cost.

LIMITS TO MONOPOLY POWER

Potential Competition

The threat of new entry hangs over monopolies like Damocles' sword. Not only does it reduce the profitability of price discrimination, it also severely restricts monopoly power in all its aspects. In a *contestable market*[21] (one with free entry and exit), the incumbent's only advantage is that of earlier entry. He expects other firms to enter if he makes excess profits. To deter such entry, he is likely to follow competitive pricing, setting P = AC, and sacrificing all supernormal profits. In a perfectly contestable market (with absolutely free entry, unlimited access to technology and resources, and totally costless exit), if a potential entrant could capture the entire market by undercutting the ruling price slightly, the only sustainable equilibrium would be at P = AC. This could occur with just a single firm in operation in the increasing returns phase of the cost curve, where the AC curve is sloping down, P = AC > MC (Fig. 6.3).

---

[21] William J. Baumol, John C. Panzar and Robert D. Willig, *Contestable Markets and the Theory of Industry Structure* (San Diego: Harcourt, Brace, Jovanovich, 1982).

Fig. 6.3: Contestable Market Monopoly

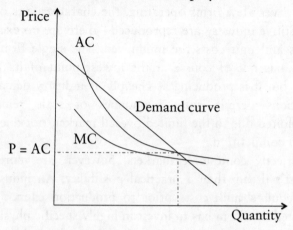

It could also occur with two or more firms in existence, each on a constant returns flat segment of the AC curve, where P = AC = MC. (Fig. 6.4).

Fig. 6.4: Contestable Market Oligopoly

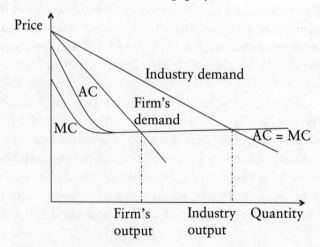

In each of these cases, despite the fact of only one, or at most, a very few firms operating, the characteristics of a competitive industry are reproduced—there are no excess profits and unit costs are minimized. The single firm in Fig. 6.3 is not of course at the lowest point of its AC curve, but it is producing as cheaply as industry demand conditions permit—some economies of scale remain unexploited due to the limited overall market, not due to lack of competition.

Perfectly contestable markets, however, are more a theorist's dream than a practical possibility. An industry that requires sunk costs prior to production cannot be contested. If a firm has to invest in highly specific physical assets, these may have to be sold at a heavy loss when the firm exits. Even if the assets are not so specific, their resale is beset by the lemons problem: they may be resalable only at prices well below their proprietary value. New entrants also need to invest in intangible assets: in information about the market they are entering, in the internal organization of their firm, in advertising to inform the consumer of their existence or to differentiate their product, and in research and development (R&D) for high-tech industry—sunk costs that would be almost entirely lost if the firm leaves the industry.

Further, it is highly implausible that an incumbent would allow his entire market to be captured by the entrant without drastic retaliation. The entrant must factor such retaliation into his calculations of the profitability of entry. It is, therefore, a threat which the incumbent can wield as a protective shield against invasion. 'Hit and run', a sudden, unexpected ambush and rapid exit before retaliation can gather momentum is the only strategy that may work if at all feasible (i.e. if entry and exit are indeed perfectly free). Given the omnipresence of sunk cost in any modern industry, that is a strategy which is only rarely implementable.

Whatever the limitations of the contestable markets model, it suggests that the most effective method of reducing monopoly power is to dismantle barriers to entry. Often, these are barriers created by the state itself, as unintended consequences of policy interventions in other areas. However, all incumbents have an incentive to limit entry, and a competition policy would perforce have to foil their designs. Examples of such entry barriers are tying arrangements (whereby sellers force buyers of a particular product to buy another unwanted product, e.g. Microsoft tying Windows with Internet Explorer in order to foreclose entry into the browser market) and resale price maintenance (whereby the seller compels distributors not to sell the product below a specified minimum price, thus restricting competition between dealers).

Durable Goods Monopoly[22]

The threat of potential competition constitutes one limit to monopoly power. A second, rather strange, source of competition arises in durable goods monopolies.

Suppose a seller has sole ownership of a *durable good* (a good which lasts for many periods and can be used to

---

[22] Ronald Coase, 'Durability and Monopoly', *Journal of Law and Economics* 15 (1972): 143–49.

provide services repeatedly). An example is a movie which is only owned by one seller and which can be screened repeatedly. The seller only faces a fixed cost in acquiring the rights to the movie. His marginal costs of showing the movie are zero (having bought the movie, he loses nothing by showing it to one more person). To maximize profits, this durable goods monopolist will equate MR = MC = 0. So he screens the movie and charges a price at which MR is equal to zero. The people most anxious to see the movie will watch it in the first period.

The demand in subsequent periods will be lower. As the demand curve shifts down, so will the MR. Though the monopolist still prices the movie such that MR = 0, this now happens at a lower and lower price. If the transaction cost of revising prices downward is small, the monopolist will indeed cut prices.

But if people foresee this, they may strategically postpone their purchase. In that case, the seller in the first period will find himself 'competing' against the spectre of himself in future periods when the good's price will be lower. Due to this competition, he will have to lower his first-period price. But every segment of consumers knows that in future he will cut prices even further—and so, apart from those who are too impatient to wait, they will continue to postpone their purchase. The seller may even have to reduce his price to the point where it just covers his cost of acquiring the movie. This is the price that will be charged in all periods, so that moviegoers have no incentive to defer their trips to the cinema. Thus, shadow-boxing with himself reduces the monopolist to the status of a perfectly competitive seller.

INTELLECTUAL PROPERTY RIGHTS AND MONOPOLY

Patents, copyrights, etc. constitute a major entry barrier. They retard the diffusion of new knowledge and thereby restrict entry into technically progressive industries. However, they create intellectual property rights, without which, it has been argued (notably by the great economist Joseph Schumpeter[23]), innovation will be a profitless business and the incentive for investment in research will vanish. There will be no new technical knowledge to diffuse, even if diffusion were perfectly free. A delicate balance needs to be struck between the requirements of rapid generation of knowledge and those of its rapid dissemination. Such a magical balancing trick is way beyond the capacity of most patent regimes. Drug patents, for example, have long been the happy hunting ground of patent legislation and litigation. Producers and consumers of generic drugs argue that the outrageous prices charged by owners of pharmaceutical patents bear no relation whatsoever to costs of production and amount in fact to trading in death. Patent holders, on the other hand, assert that drug prices should not in fact reflect the generic's minuscule costs of production but the developer's risky investment in decades of painstaking and expensive laboratory research and years of field-testing prior to release. They claim that unless these investments are recoverable, no life-saving drugs will ever be developed. Can a golden mean ever be struck between these positions? One can only wonder.

---

[23] Joseph Schumpeter, *Capitalism, Socialism and Democracy* (New York: Harper & Brothers, 1942).

SUMMARY

A monopolist is the sole producer of a good with few close substitutes. His exclusive control of his industry is sustained by a set of entry barriers. Such barriers may include sole ownership of specific indispensable resources, licences or patents or economies of scale sufficient to make it impossible for more than one firm to survive in the market. These economies of scale may be technological in nature or include network externalities or credibility issues. They pose the strongest barriers to entry when they involve large sunk costs which make both entry and exit expensive.

The monopolist maximizes profit by equating MC not to P but to MR (< P), thus restricting output below the competitive, cost-minimizing (and socially optimal) level and earning excess profits (or monopoly rent) above what he needs to stay in business. The government may seek to resolve the monopoly problem by taking it over, thus landing itself in the familiar problems of a command system with no incentive for efficiency. Or it may try to regulate the industry, especially its pricing. But if it requires marginal-cost pricing (because of social optimality considerations), the industry makes a loss and must be subsidized out of the general budget, while average-cost pricing covers cost but is socially inoptimal. Both pricing formulae erode the incentive for efficiency.

The monopolist can acquire even more power and earn more profits if it can divide its market into separable parts between which arbitrage is not possible. It can then charge higher prices in the less elastic sub-markets and lower in the more elastic ones. In the limit, it can charge a different price for each customer, extracting the entire consumer's surplus through 'all or nothing' offers. This would, of course, result in a competitive socially optimal output, but the entire surplus would be appropriated by the monopolist.

There are, however, limits to monopoly power. If a market is contestable (without barriers to entry or exit), the threat of potential competition may be as effective as actual competition in driving prices and profits down to competitive levels and minimizing unit cost. Perfect contestability however is highly unlikely, though a case can certainly be established for the dismantling of all artificial barriers to entry and exit as the best method of controlling monopoly power.

A second limit to monopoly power arises in durable goods industries where a monopolist today may have to contend with the fact that tomorrow it may be worth his while to sell his product at a lower price. This, in turn, may induce customers to delay purchase, thus creating competition between the monopolist today and the same monopolist tomorrow, a competition that may drive price down to the level of unit cost if prices can be instantaneously reduced.

Perhaps the major dilemma in the economics of monopoly relates to the role of patents. On the one hand, these restrict entry and impede the dissemination of new technology. On the other, they create and protect intellectual property rights without which the incentive to invest in research and technological progress cannot be sustained. Can we design a patent system that optimally balances these two conflicting considerations? That remains at present an open question.

PROBLEMS

1. It has sometimes been claimed that monopoly not only slows down technical progress but also actively suppresses it. To assess this issue, consider the following question. Suppose an innovation lowers the variable costs of a monopolist. What will be its impact on sales revenue? What about profits? What if it, while reducing variable cost, increases fixed cost? And what if it reduces fixed cost while not affecting variable cost?

2. A publisher pays an author a royalty amounting to 10 per cent of the sales value of a book. If both the publisher and the author are only interested in their income, would they agree on the price at which the book should be sold?

Chapter 7

Competition among the Few and Game Theory

MONOPOLISTIC COMPETITION

Between perfect competition amongst myriads of small firms and the single all-encompassing monopoly stands the world of competition among the few. However, before we enter this realm, let's visit another area of the theory of market structure.

This is monopolistic competition, so christened by the Harvard economist Edward Chamberlin in 1933.[24] Chamberlin conjured up an industry of innumerable firms, producing goods that were close, but not perfect, substitutes for each other. For example, different brands of toilet soap

---

[24] Edward Chamberlin, *The Theory of Monopolistic Competition: A Re-orientation of the Theory of Value* (Cambridge, MA: Harvard University Press, 1933).

or toothpaste. Producers in the industry *differentiated* their goods through advertising or relatively minor changes in product design and characteristics. Further, the products could not be arranged according to degrees of similarity. Firm X could not be described as closer to firm Y than to firm Z. As a consequence, the effects of the actions of X were distributed at random over the entire population of firms, so that the impact on any one was negligible and no reaction was triggered. Firm X could assume in effect that it was acting independently, just like a perfect competitor. The demand curve it faced was, however, downward sloping; it could sell a larger output only by cutting prices, but the resulting increase in its clientele was not achieved at the expense of a limited subset of rivals. Its impact was so imperceptibly dispersed over the whole industry that no one really noticed.

With a given demand curve and a corresponding given MR curve, the firm maximizes profit at MR = MC. If in this equilibrium, P > AC, excess profits are earned, new firms are attracted to the industry, and all demand curves are driven down until they become tangential to the AC curve. At the tangency output, MR would also equal MC (as shown in Chapter 4); the firm would be maximizing profits and the industry would also be in equilibrium since the maximized profits would only be the normal profits the firm needed to stay in the industry. In this long-run tangency solution, monopolistic competition will resemble perfect competition in that excess profits will be eroded away. But unlike perfect competition, it will not minimize cost but will create long-run excess capacity with equilibrium on the down-sloping segment of the AC curve. Price will also exceed MC; the value of the last unit produced will exceed its cost so that output will be socially sub-optimal. An additional unit of production will more than repay its cost to society.

Fig. 7.1: Chamberlin's Tangency Solution

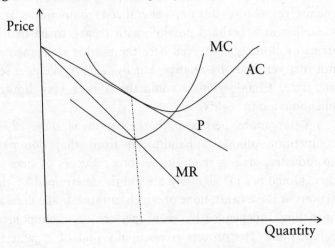

Central to the concept of monopolistic competition is the rejection of the notion of varying degrees of similarity between products. Without this, the effects of one firm's actions would be concentrated on the producers of the most similar products, the latter would per force retaliate and the first firm would have to take this retaliation into account while planning its strategy. The similarity to the competitive model would disappear and we would be transported into the world of competition among the few.

However, product differentiation rarely conforms to the Chamberlin model. Typically, the market for any product is segmented: vertically (by quality and price) and horizontally (by geography, demographics, lifestyle or by characteristics like environmental concerns). Each segment is populated by a small number of products, among which competition is intense. Competition between segments is limited. Luxury soaps compete with mass products only at the margin, while organics compete primarily among themselves. More diffuse, generalized competition a la Chamberlin is perhaps possible with regard to particular items of clothing, but even here the market is segmented not just vertically by quality, but by factors like age, sex and size. Chamberlinian competition is a very limited phenomenon in reality.

A far more pervasive market form is *oligopoly*—competition among a handful of firms that dominate an industry, among rival airlines or producers of steel or cars. Outcomes in oligopoly are jointly determined by the actions of these firms, none of which can sustain the illusion of acting independently as in perfect or monopolistic competition. The process is essentially that of a game in which the strategies of the rival players determine the end result—and an understanding of oligopoly therefore requires an introduction to the general theory of games.

GAME THEORY BASICS

Game theory analyses the actions of people in situations where these actions jointly determine the outcome of the game. The players have a choice of strategies and the outcome comprises the payoffs received by the players. The equilibrium of the game is a state in which no player has any incentive to change his strategy. Of particular importance here is the Nash equilibrium,[25] discussed earlier. A Nash

---

[25] Nash, 'Equilibrium Points', 48–9.

equilibrium is a combination of strategies from which no player has any incentive to unilaterally deviate, given the strategies of all others.

Games can be *simultaneous*—where the players move at the same time without observing each other's actions—or *sequential*—where the players move alternately (as in chess). In a sequential game, a player's strategy consists of a whole sequence of moves, each contingent on the earlier history of the game. Simultaneous games have a simpler structure with each strategy comprising just a single move; and it is these simultaneous games that will be our starting point.

NASH EQUILIBRIUM IN A SIMULTANEOUS GAME: AN EXAMPLE

An early example of a Nash equilibrium is provided by the *Bertrand duopoly*. Consider an industry with only two firms (a duopoly) producing a homogeneous product under conditions of constant identical unit cost (i.e. with MC = AC constant and equal for both firms). They compete for the market using their prices as strategies. Given any price set by firm B, firm A decides on his best response:

1. If B's price is below AC, A should stay out of the industry, since he will not be able to sell if he prices his product above B's, while if he prices it at or below B's price, he will not be able to cover costs.
2. If B charges above AC, A can slightly undercut him, thus capturing the entire market at a profitable price.
3. If B prices his product at AC, A should match his price and share the market equally, making normal, but not excess, profits as he would under perfect competition.

B does likewise, given A's prices. The two sets of strategies match if and only if both price at AC. A unilateral deviation to a higher price by one will lead to his losing the entire market; a lower price will mean that he makes losses on every unit he produces. There is a unique Nash equilibrium with the duopolists replicating the behaviour of competitive firms.

Central to any game is its *payoff matrix*. Each cell in this matrix corresponds to a particular combination of strategies, one for each player; and the entries in the cell represent the individual payoffs the players receive when they play this combination. A player's choice of strategy generally depends on his rivals' choices as well. But it is possible that a particular strategy may be best for him, regardless of what his rivals do. Such a strategy is described as a dominant strategy. If each player has a dominant strategy, the game has a *dominant strategy equilibrium*.

Box 7.1: An Example of Dominant Strategy Equilibrium: the Prisoner's Dilemma

A \ B	Cooperate	Don't cooperate
Cooperate (don't confess)	(5,5)	(-10,6)
Don't cooperate (confess)	(6,-10)	(-5,-5)

THE PRISONERS' DILEMMA

The classic example of a dominant strategy equilibrium is the *prisoners' dilemma*. Two prisoners, suspected of jointly murdering someone, are being interrogated separately. Each has the option whether to confess or not. Generally, the options are described as *cooperation* (with one's partner in crime and not with the police, i.e. not confessing) and *defection* (confession). If one of them confesses while the other does not, the confessor is released as an approver and can even grab for himself the accumulated spoils of their earlier crimes (payoff 6). His partner, poor man, is hanged (payoff -10). If both confess, they are sentenced to a life in prison (-5). But if neither confesses, there is no evidence against them: both must be released and can divide up their treasure trove between themselves (5), which is somewhat less than what either could have got if he were the sole confessor. Given this payoff matrix, each prisoner's best option is to confess, regardless of what the other does. They are doomed by dominant strategy equilibrium to live out the rest of their lives in jail, when, if neither confessed, they could both have gone scot-free. The equilibrium is very far from the Pareto-optimum.

The prisoners' dilemma haunts us everywhere. Consider arms races. Both country A and country B would prefer to spend their tax revenues in enhancing the welfare of their citizens rather than in arming themselves against each other. But if A arms and B doesn't, the latter faces the unpleasant prospect of enslavement by the former; and if A doesn't and B does, the latter finds himself in the rather enjoyable position of being able to enslave the former. Arming is clearly the dominant strategy for B; likewise for A. Hence, an arms race at the expense of the citizens of both countries.

We have already studied the instability of cartels. If the other members of my cartel restrict output, I will enjoy the benefit of a higher price for our common product even if I do not limit my production; and, of course, if they do not, my unilateral output restriction will only reduce my income without raising price. So, I will not restrict my output, nor, by the same token, will anyone else, and the cartel collapses.

The prisoners' dilemma also underlies the failure of the market to provide public goods. Each consumer of the public good reasons that if he pays for the good but others do not, the good will not be produced, while if he doesn't pay but others do, it will be supplied despite his free-riding. And, of course, by the very definition of a public good, he cannot be excluded from its benefits. Therefore, he doesn't pay, nor does anyone else. The good is not produced for the private market.

Possibly the most important illustration of the prisoners' dilemma in the analysis of oligopoly relates to competition in R&D among large firms. In almost all industries on the frontiers of technology—in computers, software, pharmaceuticals, biotechnology, aerospace and many others—most firms compete intensely in the effort to develop new products and processes. A successful innovation creates a temporary monopoly and the firm enjoys windfall profits. But these are uncertain, rare and very transient, rapidly eroded by competing innovations. Yet, if one falls behind in the technological rat race, extinction is almost certain. Investment in R&D is worthwhile, indeed imperative, whatever my competitors may be doing. This, despite the fact that long-run expected profits in these industries are rarely more than the bare minimum needed to stay in business.

THE BATTLE OF THE SEXES

Box 7.2: Equilibrium by Deletion of Dominated Strategies

Boy \ Girl	Kickboxing	Ballet
Kickboxing	(4,1)	(2,3)
Ballet	(1,1)	(3,3)

Relatively few games have a dominant strategy equilibrium. Some, however, can be solved by *deletion of dominated strategies*. Consider the following story that is not unusual. Boy meets girl and develops a crush on her. The girl, unfortunately, is indifferent to his affections. The two have a choice of attending one of two events, together or singly—a kick-boxing match or a ballet performance. The boy prefers kick-boxing if he has to go to an event by himself (payoff 2 against 1), but so infatuated is he with the girl that for the sake of her company, he would actually prefer the ballet (3 against 2). Of course, he would be happiest (4) if she happened to be at the kick-boxing match with him. The girl gets no kicks at all out of kick-boxing (1), and her preference for the ballet is entirely independent of the boy's presence or absence (3). In the circumstances, the girl's possible visit to the kick-boxing event is a dominated strategy: it can be deleted, reducing the payoff matrix to its right-hand column, with the obvious solution that both boy and girl will end up at the ballet.

Box 7.3: The Battle of the Sexes

Boy \ Girl	Kickboxing	Ballet
Kickboxing	(4,2)	(2,1)
Ballet	(0,0)	(3,3)

This saga of unrequited love is replaced by another if the girl begins to reciprocate the boy's affection. Given the strategy of the other, each retains his/her original preference, the boy for kick-boxing, the girl for ballet. However, both would prefer to watch some event together rather than apart. In this scenario, there are two equilibria, one with both at the kick-boxing arena, the other with both watching the ballet. In neither of these two situations, would either have an incentive to unilaterally deviate. Multiple equilibria, however, pose problems of their own. If the boy and the girl coordinate their plans, they can arrange to meet at one of the two possible events. But what if they are both too shy to arrange a definitive date? What if each is hoping merely to 'accidentally' run into the other? It is perfectly possible then that the boy will end up bored and forlorn at the ballet looking in vain for the girl who, meanwhile, is searching for him at the kick-boxing venue while averting her eyes from the mayhem in the arena. What one needs is coordination, either through direct communication or through an *equilibrium selection device*.

Such a game of coordination has been described, rather inappropriately, as *the battle of the sexes*. There are, however, other versions that capture more of the battlefield aura. One account tells the tale of a young, loving but very jealous couple. The husband works in an office; the wife stays home and attends to the household. Alone in her spick-and-span surroundings, she is assailed by doubts. 'I dearly love Ram and I know he adores me. But he's too weak to say "No" to anyone. How will he resist the wiles of that voluptuous secretary of his? And, if he cannot, the one role I would hate above all things to play would be that of the wronged and helpless wife.' Meanwhile, the husband has his concerns too: 'No one could have a more wonderful wife than Seeta. But surely she gets bored by being at home all day. How long can she rebuff the attentions of that handsome neighbour who keeps visiting her for cups of sugar and heaven knows what else?' For consolation, he plunges into work with his secretary. After one such hectic session has failed to allay his fears, he rushes home before time and discovers Seeta in the arms of the neighbour. 'So these are the household chores that keep you constantly busy?' he sneers. 'And what about the lipstick on your collar', she counters, 'and the mascara on your cheek?' The upshot is flying crockery, leading up to a grand finale in the divorce courts.

MULTIPLE EQUILIBRIA, CONVENTIONS AND FOCAL POINTS

Conventions can be best understood as equilibrium selection devices in games of coordination. 'All driving on the left' or 'All driving on the right' represent alternative equilibria in coordination games involving many drivers. If either of these is adopted as a convention, that would constitute a device for selecting one of the two equilibria and eliminating fatal confusion. The convention would signal to each driver what the others will do, and thereby minimize accidents.

In the absence of conventions, *focal points* (sometimes called *Schelling points* after Nobel laureate Thomas Schelling[26] who pioneered the concept in his 1960 classic *The Strategy of Conflict*) are often helpful in selecting between equilibria. A focal point is an object whose natural salience causes people to focus on it. Two visitors to New York City have made an appointment to meet, but communication between them has somehow been disrupted before they could specify a time and place. How would they coordinate their plans? Experiments show that a high proportion would opt for a noon visit to the top of the Empire State Building in the expectation that their friend would do likewise. Many such focal points exist. An overwhelming majority of those asked to choose between heads and tails (in a game in which people are rewarded if their choice matches their partner's) choose heads. A large proportion of those asked to pick a particular number (under similar conditions) chooses one. Focal points differ between different groups of players according to culture and history, but they are crucial in resolving coordination problems in the choice between alternative equilibria.

ZERO-SUM GAMES

The polar opposite of the game of pure coordination is the two-person *zero-sum game*. In these, one player's loss is the other's gain so that the payoffs of the players add up to zero

---

[26] Thomas Schelling, *The Strategy of Conflict* (Cambridge: Harvard University Press, 1960).

and their interests are in direct conflict. With three or more players, the conflict aspect of the game gets blurred because it is always possible for two of the players to team up against the third, so that coalitional and cooperative considerations enter the players' calculations.

In the two-person zero-sum game, I maximize my payoff by minimizing my opponent's. According to the postulates of game theory, I also credit my opponent with enough intelligence to do the same to me. So the value of any strategy to me is represented by the minimum payoff that I could earn by employing that strategy. The strategy I adopt will be the one that offers me the highest of these minimized payoffs. It is my *maximin* strategy. My opponent adopts his maximin strategy. If my strategy matches his— if, that is, I am maximizing my payoff subject to his strategy at the same time that he is minimizing my payoff subject to my strategy. We then have an equilibrium: a minimax equilibrium. Neither of us would want to unilaterally deviate.

Box 7.4: A Maximin Solution

A \ B	Choose low price (Re 1)	Choose high price (Rs 2)
Choose low price (Re 1)	(0,0)	(500,-500)
Choose high price (Rs 2)	(-500,500)	(0,0)

As an example, imagine an industry with a unit-elastic demand curve. Its total sales revenue is constant at all prices (due to sales volume changing in inverse proportion as price changes). Suppose this constant sales revenue is 1000. There are two firms in the industry, each with fixed costs of 500 and zero variable cost. The firms are constrained to choose between two prices: one low (1), the other high (2). If they choose the same price, they share the market equally, earn a sales revenue of 500 and make zero profits. But if one charges the high price and the other the low, the latter captures the entire market and earns a profit of 500 while the firm that demanded the high price makes a loss of 500. If I charge the high price, the worst that can happen to me is -500, while if I charge the low price, I cannot do worse than 0. So I opt for the low price. My opponent uses the same reasoning to reach the same conclusion. Both of us charge a low price.

Fig. 7.2: Hotelling's Problem

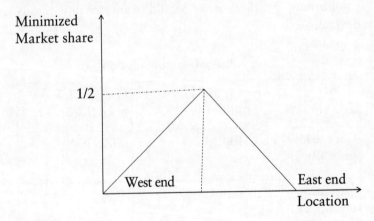

Among the best-known minimax equilibria is the solution to Hotelling's problem. Harold Hotelling, in a 1929 paper, visualized two grocers coming into what was essentially a Wild West town comprising a single long street (somewhat unnecessarily named Main Street) with consumers distributed uniformly along it. The grocers cannot compete in product choice, price or quality (perhaps these are prescribed by the municipality); the only dimension in which they can compete is location. The consumers are lazy; they buy from whichever shop is nearest. Now, given grocer A's location, grocer B's best response can be formulated as follows:

1. If A locates to the east of the midpoint of Main Street, B will locate immediately to his west, thus capturing the entire market to the west of A, which is more than half the total market and leaving to A only what lies to his east.

2. If A locates to the west of the midpoint, B will position himself immediately to his east, leaving to A only that fraction of the total market (less than half) that lies to his west.

3. If A locates at the midpoint, B can do no better than locate just across the street opposite him. Consumers will now be indifferent between them and will distribute themselves at random between A and B. The two will share the market equally.

Since A credits B with enough intelligence to always make his best response, A can do no better than to locate at the midpoint. B reasons similarly and does likewise. A minimax equilibrium at the midpoint of Main Street is reached.

Hotelling's problem has been applied in a wide variety of contexts, most notably in the analysis of democratic politics. In these more general applications, the midpoint equilibrium needs to be reinterpreted as a median solution (one where the number of consumers to one's left is exactly equal to the number on one's right). Where consumers are uniformly distributed, this coincides with the median.

An obvious application is to the case of two-party election contests. Wherever the preferences of the electorate can be represented along a linear spectrum (say from the political Left to the political Right), and contestants define their positions along this spectrum with the sole objective of winning the election, the parallel to the Hotelling problem is exact. Voters will vote for the candidate or party closest to their personal positions on the spectrum, the contestants will converge to the position of the median voter, each will get almost the same vote as the other and winning will be a matter of luck.

Is there real-world evidence of all this? Certainly, in countries with two dominant political parties, the common complaint is that there is no genuine difference between the parties, one is simply offered a choice between Tweedledum and Tweedledee, and a bipartisan policy consensus is imposed on the country. Evidence of policy convergence and of the median voter theorem is not too difficult to come by.

What about the theorem's predictions regarding voting figures? Possibly, the US presidential elections offer the best testing ground for these. The elections are dominated by the candidates of two major parties with negligible presence of anybody else. Most voters have well-defined positions on the Left–Right spectrum, the candidates (at least most of them) want passionately to win and adopt their stated positions accordingly. There are, of course, exceptions to the circumstances postulated in the theorem—crucial issues that lie outside the Left–Right spectrum or candidates who are passionate about things other than winning. However, it is interesting that the elections have sometimes produced nearly identical vote counts. Kennedy versus Nixon, 1960, saw Kennedy win the popular vote by a margin of just 0.17 per cent. Vote fraud by Chicago mayor Daley's political machine in Cook County and by Lyndon Johnson's political machine in Texas is often credited with the Kennedy victory. Bush versus Gore, 2000, actually saw the electoral college loser Gore winning the popular vote by a margin of 0.5 per cent; and here it has been claimed that the decision of the conservative Supreme Court stopping a recount in Florida (which Bush was declared to have won by a few hundred votes) was what determined the outcome.

But what if a contestant is more interested in making an ideological point than winning? Before the 1964 elections, a faction, which could be called the rabid Right by the standards of those days, captured the Republican Party. It sought to differentiate its product sharply from that of the Democrats, and in the process, its presidential candidate, Barry Goldwater, carved out a niche for himself somewhere in the middle of the national right wing. The Democrats, meanwhile, continued to target the median voter. The consequences were predictable. Goldwater won the votes of the 25 per cent to his Right and the 12.5 per cent between his position and Johnson's. The rest of the country voted Democratic in the greatest electoral landslide in US history. One could have predicted a 62.5–37.5 split. The actual figures were 61 per cent to 37 per cent with 2 per cent voting for 'also-rans'.

MIXED STRATEGIES AND THE MINIMAX THEOREM

Many zero-sum games do not have a minimax solution in pure strategies. However, the great mathematician John von Neumann[27] proved that every such game has a solution in *mixed strategies*—where each player plays each of his strategies randomly but with a predetermined probability. To illustrate, consider the game of *matching pennies*. In this game, players Ram and Seeta each have a penny and may secretly turn these to either heads or tails. They then simultaneously disclose their choices. If they match (both heads or both tails), Ram gets both pennies for a gain of 1 while Seeta gets -1. If there is no such match, Seeta gets both pennies. There is no pure strategy equilibrium, since whatever one chooses, the other can always reduce him or her to -1 by an appropriate choice of strategy. Suppose, however, that each decides to choose heads or tails with equal probability ½. Then each of the four possible outcomes of the game will occur with a probability of ¼, and the expected payoff of each player will be 0, which, if not spectacular, is at least better than the pure strategy alternative of -1. If Ram decides to show heads with a probability higher than ½, Seeta can reduce his expected payoff (and improve hers) by showing tails. If he shows heads with probability less than ½, she could show heads, with the same results. Only a probability of ½ will ensure an expected outcome of 0. Exactly symmetrical reasoning explains why Seeta too would randomize between her strategies with a probability of ½.

---

[27] John von Neumann and Oskar Morgenstern, *The Theory of Games and Economic Behaviour* (Princeton: Princeton University Press, 1944).

Box 7.5: A Game with No Pure Strategy Equilibrium: Matching Pennies

A \ B	Head	Tail
Head	(1,-1)	(-1,1)
Tail	(-1,1)	(1,-1)

There is a famous empirical test of the minimax theorem involving penalty kicks in soccer.[28] There are three strategies that a penalty-kicker may employ, to shoot straight, or to the goalkeeper's right or to his left. The goalkeeper also has three strategies, to stay in the middle or to dive to his right or to his left. This is a zero-sum game: the objectives of the two players are directly opposed. Analysing data from hundreds of soccer matches, Chiappori, Levitt and Groseclose show that penalty kickers and goalkeepers behave as von Neumann had predicted. The minimax theorem is alive and kicking on the football field.

REPEATED GAMES

All the games described so far have been single-shot affairs. But most of the transactions and encounters in real life are

[28] Pierre-André Chiappori, Steven Levitt and Timothy Groseclose, 'Testing Mixed Strategy Equilibria when Players are Heterogeneous: The Case of Penalty Kicks in Soccer', *American Economic Review* 92 (2002): 1138–51.

repeated, often endlessly. To make sense of reality, therefore, we need a theory of repeated games.

When a game is repeated indefinitely, its outcome often changes. For example, if the prisoners' dilemma is repeated, the players know that, when one of them defects, the others can retaliate by defecting over the periods that follow. Would the threat of such retaliation deter potential defectors? Unfortunately not, if the game has a definite end. Last-period defectors face no threat of retaliation because there is no tomorrow. Everyone defects in the last period. But then, the threat of retaliation is meaningless in the second-last period as well, since I know that my opponent will defect anyway in future. In consequence, everyone defects in the second-last period too. And so on . . . until through backward induction we reach the present. A finite repeated game simply repeats the conclusion of the single-shot game that defection is inevitable.

Things are very different if the game is indefinitely repeated. Since there is now no definite last period, there is no last-period problem. The threat of future retaliation is real and credible. The worst-case scenario would be a threat of defection over the indefinite future, a 'grim' retaliatory strategy, so called because it is certainly no laughing matter for either of the parties involved. When someone contemplates defecting, he must balance the present gains from doing so against the losses due to retaliation thereafter. His calculations are profoundly affected by the degree of his impatience, the rate at which he discounts the future. If the future means nothing to him, he will not be deterred by any threat of future loss. But if he is not quite so myopic, deterrence is certainly possible. For any rate of discount, one can work out the present value of the losses that the potential defector would incur over the indefinite future. If this exceeds the gains from defection, no one will defect. For a low enough rate of discount, this will always happen (since losses over the indefinite future will then add up to match or exceed any given present gain from defection), a well-known result of obscure origin which, for that reason, is called the folk theorem of game theory.

Of course, such a threat is not costless to the person making it. The threat would be credible if and only if the cost to him of implementing it is less than the losses he would suffer from his opponent's defection.

If both these conditions are fulfilled, the indefinitely repeated game will have a cooperative solution.

There are other retaliatory strategies that are not quite so grim. One could retaliate by defecting for a finite number of periods, possibly for just long enough to deter. If deterrence is possible in finite time, it would be pointless to threaten a longer period of retaliation. It would not be credible either, since defection is costly. One could also play tit-for-tat, starting with first-period cooperation and thereafter replicating the opponent's previous-period behaviour.

Anyway, indefinitely repeated games form a powerful defence, firmly founded on individual self-interest, against uncooperative behaviour.

SEQUENTIAL GAMES

In contrast to all the earlier games, in which the players move simultaneously, a sequential game is one in which one player moves first and the others respond. To illustrate, suppose a single incumbent firm I monopolizes a market into which a new entrant E is contemplating entry. There are no external barriers to entry.

In the first stage of the game, E decides whether to enter or not. If he stays out, the game terminates with I earning monopoly profit and E earning 0. If he enters, a new stage of the game begins. The incumbent I must now decide whether to fight the entrant through a costly price war or to accommodate him. The possible strategies in the game with their payoffs can be shown in the form of a game tree.

Fig. 7.3: Game Tree

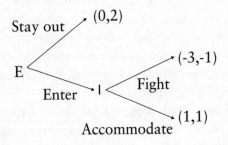

To solve such a sequential game, one must figure out what will happen in the last stage and then work backwards (backward induction). In this case:

1. If E believed I's threat of fighting, E would not enter as he would be much worse off in a fight (-3) than by not entering at all (0).
2. But E can work out that I's threat is empty (not credible). If E does enter, I gets more by accommodating him—getting 1—than by engaging in a costly price war, which gives the incumbent -1.

3. So E can ignore this threat and assume that if he enters, I will accommodate him. As E's payoff from entering and being accommodated is higher than his payoff from not entering, he will enter.

So, the equilibrium is that E enters and I accommodates him. Though a Nash equilibrium, this equilibrium has the additional property of ruling out empty threats. Such an equilibrium is called a *subgame-perfect Nash equilibrium*.

BERTRAND REVISITED AS A SEQUENTIAL GAME

We could reconstruct the behaviour of Bertrand duopolists as a sequential game to generate a curious example of a subgame-perfect Nash equilibrium. Recall that the equilibrium of the one-off game involved competitive pricing, equal market sharing and zero excess profits. Now, imagine that the players set prices sequentially, but in an open-ended sequence. Imagine also that each can respond instantly to any price set by his opponent, as indeed he can in the age of the Internet.

Under these assumptions, there is a unique subgame-perfect Nash equilibrium, but it occurs not at the competitive, but at the monopoly price! If I charge the monopoly price, my opponent could undercut me but would find me retaliating instantly by undercutting him except when he sets the competitive price (which I would match but not undercut). The best he could do by undercutting me would be to earn zero excess profit. On the other hand, if he matched the monopoly price, he could share the market and the monopoly profit equally with me. Thus, any threat of undercutting would not be credible. Both players would charge the monopoly price and divide the market equally between themselves.

PROBLEMS

1. An industry which is unable to compete with imports is lobbying the government for protection. It argues that it is an 'infant industry', that with some initial help it will be able to invest in quality improvement and cost reduction to compete effectively in the future, at which time the protection could be withdrawn. Whether it actually gets protection depends on the political balance of power, which is not expected to change in the foreseeable future. You are a dispassionate and impartial observer. Using only game-theoretic arguments, give your opinion on whether the industry should be given protection or not.

2. Investors want to invest only in firms that won't cheat them. They can verify if their firm is cheating them from balance sheets, dividend payments, etc., but only after a lag. So, in order to attract investors, firms hire auditors whom the investors trust—the auditors inspect their accounts and certify whether the firm is acting honestly or not. If the auditor's certificate is not borne out subsequently by the balance sheet etc., the auditor loses the trust of all investors forever. Suppose now that an auditor, just before submitting his audit report, blackmails his firm. He threatens to submit a false report that the firm is cheating unless he is paid a bribe (in addition to the contractual fee). Would the firm pay the bribe? Explain in game-theoretic terms.

3. Your game theory professor this semester has asked all students to come well-prepared for every class. 'You may be in for a nasty surprise test any day,' he warns. You know that your professor is a stickler for accurate use of language and that he does everything according to the rules of game theory. Would you be alarmed by his threat? Does this problem show that game theory doesn't have all the answers?

PART II

PART II

Introduction

We have, up to this point, been concerned only with *micro-economics*, with the affairs of individuals and firms, in isolation or, occasionally, in interaction. We have examined their behaviour when they believe themselves to be acting independently, under perfect or monopolistic competition or even monopoly. We have looked at some of the much less predictable, more wayward ways, of interacting oligopolists. The question remains, however, of the *macro-economy*—how all this adds up for the economy as a whole. What, if anything, can we predict about the ways in which large aggregates of individuals and firms behave?

This remains a relevant and unresolved question, partly because of what Keynes described as the fallacy of composition—the false belief that what is true of the parts is necessarily true of the whole. We shall come across examples of this fallacy in later chapters. Of course, as recent research in macro-economics has emphasized, no macro-economic theory can be valid unless it is derived from sound micro-economic logic, which is why micro-economics occupies by far the larger part of this book.

However, there are other reasons why a study of aggregative behaviour is essential. A key issue throughout this book is the relationship between the market and the state, and the state's primary concern is with aggregates. It is with reference to these aggregates that the state sets its objectives and decides its instruments since collective behaviour is the stuff of public policy. And it is not only the state that influences and manipulates the collective behaviour of the private actors in the economy. What takes place, in fact, is a game of mutual interaction between the state and the public at large in which all the players look for aggregative signals of how they are performing. Is the country better off? Has unemployment declined? Are prices rising, falling or stable? How does our economic condition compare with that of the rest of the world or indeed with that of our forefathers? We need measures and indices to answer these questions and a theory to assess the impact, if any, of policy. And it is an understanding of these issues that we will next try to achieve.

Chapter 8

National Income: Measurement and Meaning

THE CIRCULAR FLOW OF INCOME

Probably the most important of all macroeconomic indices is *national income* (NI). National income can be thought of as a circular flow of money income (wages, interest, profit, and rent) from firms to households and of money expenditure on final goods and services from households to firms. Alternatively, it can be thought of as a reverse flow of the services of real inputs (labour, capital, land) from households to firms and real outputs from firms to households. The money flows represent payments for the real goods and services.

Fig. 8.1: The Circular Flow of Income

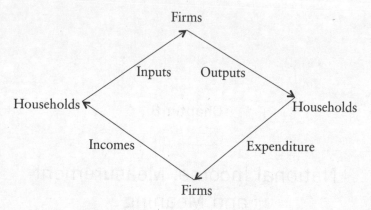

The implications are:

1. that NI does not include transfer payments—flows that do not pay for any real good or service (e.g. charity, unemployment compensation, gifts).
2. that it does not include expenditure on intermediate goods (their cost is included in the value of final goods and services: so the inclusion of intermediates as well as final goods would mean double counting).

In an open economy, there are four slightly different versions of NI: gross national product (GNP), net national product (NNP), gross domestic product (GDP), and net domestic product (NDP). The difference between national and domestic product reflects that between all that is produced by our nationals, whether at home or abroad, and all that is produced within our borders, whether by our nationals or foreigners. National product excludes the earnings of foreigners in our country but includes those of our nationals abroad. Domestic product includes the former but excludes the latter. Gross and net product differ along another dimension altogether—both gross and net product measure all that is produced currently but gross product makes no deduction for replacement of depreciated assets while net product does so.

National income thus defined is a monetary value. This is a source of several issues. Except for a person afflicted by midas mania, money by itself confers no real benefit. What matters is the command it represents over real goods and services. But the real value of money, its purchasing power, differs over space and time. So, if we are using national income for intertemporal comparisons, if we are investigating its growth or decline, we must deflate the national income figures by an index of prices. Even this would not suffice for international comparisons. Even at the same point of time, prices in different countries when converted to a common currency bear little relationship to each other. Exchange rates are dominated by volatile flows of speculative portfolio investment and diverge widely from *purchasing power parities*. Even if such short-term speculation had not been the main determinant of exchange rates, one would have to take into account the fact that the world market for tradable goods and services is deeply fragmented by transport costs and trade restrictions while for the vast range of non-tradables, there is very little correlation between prices worldwide. So, national income figures can be compared only after processing price indices and purchasing power parities. And, as we have indicated in an earlier chapter, these indices have enormous biases built in.

National income, of course, is an aggregative measure for the population as a whole. Often, we are interested primarily in the average man, in his productivity and his standard of living, and to assess these we need measures per head of the population. Per capita income was long regarded as the prime measure of the average well-being of a society and the prime indicator of its development.

Measures of development serve two distinct functions. First, they represent yardsticks for international comparison. They have as such a cross-sectional dimension and reflect international inequalities, presumably in the degree of 'well-being' of different societies worldwide. Second, they have a time-series aspect—they chronicle the progress of any particular society over time, again in terms of its 'well-being'. Typically, the same measure is used for both these purposes—a measure of this intangible well-being. However, the parameters available for a cross-sectional comparison are different from those on which a time-series analysis can be based, so that different criteria can, and perhaps should, be employed for the two cases. I shall return to this theme later.

PROBLEM

1. Which of the following are part of national income and why (or why not)? If any of them is part of national income, classify it as GDP, GNP, NDP or NNP. Remember that any particular item may be part of more than one measure of national income.

   a) The value of chillies grown by Madhvi in her kitchen garden for the consumption of her family and friends.

   b) The income of Japanese executives at the Maruti plant in Gurgaon.

c) The expenditure on the repair and maintenance of the Taj Mahal.

d) Unemployment compensation.

e) The value of cloth which the government produces and gifts to needy families who use it to make garments for sale.

f) A thief's earnings from thievery.

DOES NATIONAL INCOME MEASURE OUTPUT OR WELL-BEING?

What does national income really measure? One claim is that it measures the size or volume of a country's output. How can such a measure be constructed in a multi-good economy in which different goods grow at different rates and sometimes even in different directions? If a country produces only butter and guns and if butter output today has risen by 20 per cent while output of guns has declined by 5 per cent, how much has total output grown? Indeed, has it grown or declined? To get a composite measure of the aggregate, we need to weight different products appropriately. And most such weighting schemes are arbitrary. A non-arbitrary scheme would be to weight different goods according to the value that the consumer puts on them (i.e. the price he is prepared to pay for them). The justification for weighting each good by its value to the consumer is that goods are economically important only in proportion to their value to the consumer. But then the national income figure that we derive is essentially a measure of consumer well-being. No other independent and non-arbitrary measurement of the volume of an economy's output is possible.

If population is changing, per capita income may be a better measure of individual welfare than aggregate income.

There are, however, major problems with interpreting per capita income as an index of welfare:

1. The first of these is the *income distribution problem*. In an unequal society, the variation in individual income and welfare about the average blurs the value of per capita income as a measure of welfare. One could, of course, use a measure of the degree of income equality as a supplement to per capita income. But one would then have to ask what relative weightage should one assign to equality and to per capita income—a question to which all answers are necessarily arbitrary and loaded with personal prejudice.

2. Equally intractable is the *index number problem* which, as we have seen in Chapter 4, creates upward or downward biases in any measure of income growth.

3. A common and major criticism of the use of national income indices relates to the *imputation problem*—of imputing arbitrary values to goods that do not enter the market (and so have no price weights attached to them). Some of these goods are bartered but never enter the circle of monetary exchange. Some are produced for self-consumption—this includes not just production for subsistence but also services performed within the household, by housewives or children for example. It also includes activities (or inactivity) that yield no material output but give rise to satisfaction nevertheless (such as leisure). There is also the entire class of public goods— goods that cannot be produced for the private market because it is technologically impossible to restrict their

use to paying customers alone. Public goods may be natural resources or producible goods, anything, in fact, to which access is prohibitively costly (or impossible) to restrict—the atmosphere, the environment, defence, law and order, flood control, civic hygiene, pollution control, public health and much else. All these contribute to well-being. Many are indispensable for life itself. Yet the imputation of prices to them is totally arbitrary and generally inadequate.

4. Not quite so well known is the *stock-flow problem*. National income measures flows, but well-being is often the consequence of the enjoyment of durable stocks (e.g. the body, the environment, housing, etc.), which are reflected in national income only to the extent that they depreciate and require maintenance expenditure. Thus, medical expenditure on curing diseases and healing injuries adds to national income, good health and safety do not. Expenditure on food contributes to national income not only if it alleviates hunger but also if it merely nurtures obesity. In fact, in the latter case, it contributes doubly since it induces the cardio-vascular problems that compel more medical expenditure. Earthquakes and large-scale fires result in housing booms that add to GDP (and to NDP unless a replacement allowance of 100 per cent is deducted). Do they really increase well-being?

5. Even if all these problems are somehow miraculously solved, there remains the quite intractable *aspirations problem*—a given basket of goods may yield very different levels of welfare in societies that aspire to different standards of consumption. It may yield very different levels of welfare in a given society before and

after that society has been exposed to the *demonstration effect* of richer economies.

PROBLEMS

1. National income figures are said to underestimate the level and overestimate the rate of growth of income in poor countries. Why?
2. The government of Banana Republic is very concerned about the opinion of a group of voters called the Mango people. It feels it is becoming unpopular with them because the national income figures it publishes show negative growth. It hires Dr Too Smart, the statistical wizard at PKU, to take care of the problem. He succeeds in doing the job without cooking the raw data. How do you think he did it?

ASPIRATIONS AND WELL-BEING

Perhaps one should elaborate a bit on the last of these problems because it is the least familiar. Traditionally, economic growth is said to be correlated with increased welfare on the assumption of stability of tastes. But almost all growth processes are accompanied, and most are set off, by changes in preferences. Typically, the initiating factor is a 'revolution of rising aspirations', a rise in the desire for material goods and services generated by exposure to the example of advanced living standards elsewhere. But then we can no longer interpret economic growth in terms of an increase in welfare. The higher consumption standards of development may yet leave people more dissatisfied than ever.

A counterargument to this asserts that mankind shares a common pattern of underlying needs. As we grow, our tastes develop from these common needs by adapting to whatever is possible. We do not yet want the moon, however intense our underlying passion for it may be. However, as scientific and economic development widens our horizon of possibilities, the inhibitions on our desires due to knowledge of the limits of possibility recede and more and more of the structure of our basic needs is revealed and may then be satisfied. In short, the more recent a taste pattern, the more accurate a representation it is of our underlying wants. The newer preferences were present but latent earlier and have simply surfaced because of the widening of the range of possibilities. We may always have wanted to gossip interminably while doing everything else but never even considered the possibility before the invention of the cell phone. Therefore, if people today prefer their current living standards (as evident from the fact that they have chosen them) to the standards they experienced earlier, they must now be better off.

This theory is based on two postulates. The first is the claim that an unconscious taste pattern underlies our conscious preferences. Modern psychology unfortunately provides no support for such a belief. Our subliminal impulses do not constitute a rational ordering with the standard properties of completeness, consistency, transitivity etc. discussed in Chapter 4. They comprise rather a chaos of unresolved conflicts on which a modicum of order has somehow been imposed by the learning processes of life, and this order is limited to the conscious layers of the mind. Below the surface lies a volcano of explosive impulses ready to erupt at the touch of experience in forms totally unrelated to our conscious scales of preference. Exposure to psychotropic drugs, for example, induces behaviour that has no link whatsoever with pre-existing wants. Mass exposure may create appetites that are then justified and rationalized into new systems of values and preference patterns like the drug counter-culture of the seventies or the opium habit of nineteenth-century China. Addictions and revolutions of rising expectations both result from exposure to new consumption patterns and both modify tastes and behaviour. As many remonstrating parents of the hippies and beatniks of the seventies discovered, one cannot logically distinguish between the two. Indeed, gurus of the drug counter-culture from Aldous Huxley to Carlos Castaneda have argued that addictions are profound learning experiences, that drugs heighten awareness, that mescaline or peyote (or LSD) open the doors of perception and give access to 'a separate reality' from which the uninitiated have the misfortune to be excluded. We cannot reject the Huxley–Castaneda thesis if we believe that education enables us to know ourselves (and not just the outside world), not unless we make a paternalistic decision in favour of certain kinds of experiences and instincts and against others.

The second postulate is that people today have all the options they enjoyed earlier and, thanks to economic growth and technological progress, some more. This, of course, is a gross over-simplification. I may love nothing more than walking or cycling to work but the distances I have to travel in a modern urban-industrial economy simply rule this out. My passion for the close personal contact and personalized entertainment of agrarian societies cannot be fulfilled by the press and electronic media that have replaced them. I may want my fruit fresh from the bough, my vegetables fresh from the field, and my fish fresh from the river or sea, but this can only be a pipe dream in an economy where vast distances and long delays separate production and consumption. I love open spaces and greenery but am constrained to live out my days in a high-rise amid the congestion and pollution of the urban sprawl. In short, the world has changed. Even if the world as a whole could have turned back the clock and returned to where it was a century or even a decade ago (should it have preferred that), no individual can do so. He simply doesn't have the choice. He is trapped in a Nash equilibrium from which there is no escape. The argument that he has chosen this and hence must be better off than he was is very wide off the mark.

THE EMPIRICAL EVIDENCE

Evidently, per capita income is a very poor index of welfare. Nor is this only a theoretical possibility. Direct evidence of the mismatch between per capita income and perceptions of well-being is abundant. In the seventies, various polling agencies conducted opinion surveys worldwide on the self-assessed degree of happiness of people in different societies. Examining the evidence in an influential paper, Richard Easterlin[29] posed the question: 'Does economic growth improve the human lot?' and answered it resoundingly in the negative. The surveys disclosed no cross-sectional

---

[29] Richard Easterlin, 'Does Economic Growth Improve the Human Lot? Some Empirical Evidence', in *Nations and Households in Economic Growth: Essays in Honor of Moses Abramovitz*, ed. Paul A. David and Melvin W. Reder (New York: Academic Press, 1974).

relationship whatsoever between per capita income and the average degree of happiness of any society. The happiest societies, in fact, seem to be those in the remote hinterlands of continents out of touch with modern civilization.

Possibly more dramatic even than the Easterlin Paradox is the evidence of the suicide rates. The suicide rate, the rate of preference for death over life, is the most irrefutable behavioural index of unhappiness. Yet, the rankings of countries by suicide rate are strongly and significantly correlated with their rankings by per capita income. The richer your country, the more likely are you to kill yourself.

The popular explanation of all such anomalies runs in terms of income distribution. If well-being depends less on absolute income than on one's relative income status, and if richer societies are also more unequal, they could well be more miserable and suicide-prone. Unfortunately, the evidence contradicts this explanation even more emphatically. Before the dissolution of the socialist world, the very high suicide rates of the Soviet Union and eastern Europe were sometimes explained as reflecting the rate at which the secret police pushed people off roofs and reported that they had jumped to their deaths. But the link between equality and suicide extended well beyond socialism and indeed outlasted it. National suicide rates today remain strongly negatively correlated to standard inequality measures—the more egalitarian a country, the keener are its citizens to embrace death.

ALTERNATIVE MEASURES: THE HUMAN DEVELOPMENT INDEX

Whatever the explanation of this mystery, it is apparent that per capita income growth does not necessarily enhance welfare. Can we design an alternative index that does a better job of tracking changes in welfare? Perhaps if our measure of development assigned less weight to material consumption and more to 'empowerment' indices such as health and education, the paradox would be resolved. Amartya Sen[30] has developed a *capabilities approach* to the question of relative levels of well-being that focuses on the capacity of people to function effectively in various spheres of life. The human development index (HDI), inspired largely by Sen's work, highlights three aspects of life: longevity, education, and the standard of living. More subtle criteria of capability have also been designed. All such measures however emphasize, in addition to life, liberty and per capita income, various components of health, education and gender equality.

When the relative performance of the different Indian states is gauged by these yardsticks, one state, Kerala, emerges as the clear winner on all counts except that of per capita income. It has the highest life expectancy, the lowest infant and maternal mortality, the best public health facilities, the highest literacy, the best performance in almost all educational indices, the best gender ratio, the best record in female education, health and empowerment and the lowest total fertility. With such a record of performance in areas regarded by outstanding thinkers as crucial to the quality of life, Keralites must surely enjoy the most satisfying lives among all Indians. Right?

Wrong. Kerala also has the highest rate of suicide among all states, no less than three times the national average. It

---

[30] Amartya Sen, 'Development as Capability Expansion', *Journal of Development Planning* 19 (1989): 41–58.

has the highest rate of alcoholism and possibly the highest rate of drug addiction. Instead of living in idyllic happiness relative to all other states, the population of Kerala brims over with a seething discontent with their lives that far exceeds the levels of dissatisfaction reached in any other state of the country. No doubt, the authors of the capabilities approach and the HDI were only summing up the factors that, according to their values (and those of many others), seemed highly desirable ethically. They were not creating a prescription for happiness. But should a highly successful application of their prescription (whatever its aims) have been associated with unhappiness of this intensity?

Remember too that Kerala does not represent an accidental aberration. The world over, the ranking of countries by suicide rates, averaged over any reasonable length of time, are significantly and strongly correlated with their rankings by HDI. The more empowered your country is in terms of 'human development', the likelier are you to kill yourself.

It has sometimes been argued that one needs a certain level of awareness to really plumb the depths of one's unhappiness. It is only through information about and exposure to all that life could be that we realize how truly miserable we are. The Happy Savage, sheltered in blissful ignorance, would not dream of committing suicide. But expose such savages to other ways of living before returning them irrevocably to savagery and they would kill themselves in droves.

Of course, this still does not explain why, after the Danish government began developing Greenland into a modern welfare state on the Danish model with schools, medical facilities and government-built apartment blocks, the suicide rate shot up from zero in 1960 to the highest in the world with one in every four people having attempted suicide some time during their lives. Not unless one assumes that superior awareness and exposure intensify aspirations many times more than they increase incomes or, for that matter, human development. Nor does it explain why the Danes themselves could control their own surging suicide rates only by the world's highest rates of anti-depressant use.

WHAT, IF NOT WELL-BEING?

Perhaps we should accept Easterlin's results and the suicide data at face value, rather than seek to explain them away. Perhaps prosperity or human development do not add to happiness, and economic growth does not improve the human lot. What then does it improve? What is it that grows in historical processes that we all recognize as 'growth'? The one invariable characteristic of all such processes is not an increase in well-being or even in production (which cannot be unambiguously measured when, as in all growth processes, some outputs expand and others contract); it is an improvement in biological indices, notably in life expectancy. Is biology then what lies at the back of our minds when we speak of 'economic' growth? Could life expectancy be the one true measure of development?

The view that biological improvement, an increase in a society's capacity to support life, is the essence of growth changes one's perspective on the economy. Societies must adapt to support growing numbers without disastrous increases in mortality. Poor agrarian societies, for instance, must industrialize and urbanize. The complex problems of urban-industrial life, in turn, compel innumerable adaptations. Modern transport, for instance, simply meets the mobility requirements of industrialization. Modern communications link people who would never have been separated in a less modern society. The media and the entertainment industry fill the void left by the disappearance of the personal ties and the personalized entertainment of rural life. Food processing is necessitated by the separation of production from consumption, urban construction, civic amenities and public health facilities by urban congestion.

Most of the GDP of an advanced society is a compulsion, not a net addition to welfare. Perhaps another compulsion is an increase in isolation, alienation and suicide.

When we seek to chronicle the development of a closed society over time, we cannot invoke people's perceptions of relative levels of well-being for two reasons. First, memories of the past tend to be too clouded by nostalgia or amnesia to be relied upon. Second, there is no time machine that people can ride back into the past even if they wanted to so as to reveal their preference for an older way of life. We cannot meaningfully assert that people are better (or worse) off today than they were in the past. We could use the HDI to claim that people are more (or less) 'developed' according to the values and judgement of several eminent thinkers. But this would be a paternalistic judgement with no link whatsoever to the perceptions of the people whose development we claim to be assessing. If, on the other hand, we use the capacity of a society to support life (as reflected by life expectancy or, where life expectancy is constant, by population size) as the indicator of growth, we will at least have the sanction of Darwinian evolution, which governs the development of all living species. Of course, this would still have no implications for welfare at all.

There is, however, another function that per capita income or the HDI are often used to fulfil. They are supposed to serve as yardsticks for international comparison, and here people have a very definite way of revealing their preferences. They can vote with their feet. One does not need a time machine to migrate. The net immigration rate reflects the judgement of people the world over about the attractiveness of life in any particular country. Of course, due to transport costs and migration restrictions, it is only a shadowy reflection. Where transport is expensive and migration difficult, the flow of people from one country to another understates the differences in their relative levels of development. However, the direction of net movement is an unmistakable pointer to their relative ranks. The influx of immigrants from Bangladesh indicates that India is a more developed country. The queues outside the US embassy in New Delhi reflect the development lag of India behind the US. India's attraction for migrants and invaders in ancient and medieval times proves our high economic status in those ages just as our desperate contemporary search for relocation westward demonstrates the reversal of fortune that we have suffered. Long-term net migration tells us more about how people in general (as distinct from economists) rank life in different countries than any measure of per capita income or human development would do. And life-expectancy trends tell us more about growth in a given society than all the time-profiles of per capita GDP or HDI.

Chapter 9

Macro-Economic Equilibrium

The problems of the micro-economy, of individuals and firms that act by and large on the assumption that the behaviour of others or the values of parameters like prices will not change have been explored in the first part of this book. Much of the popular interest in economics stems, however, from the phenomenon of herd behaviour—when crowds of individuals or firms act en masse, resulting in major changes in aggregates like national income, output, the price level or the degree of total unemployment. The problems of herd behaviour are especially intractable because they cannot be insured against. Since people are not acting independently, the risks they face are closely correlated; the law of averages that insurance depends on does not work. This is the stuff of macro-economics, and, though based on the micro-foundations already explored, it uses tools and concepts that are quite distinctive.

The basic problem of macro-economics is that of a disequilibrium between the supply of aggregate output and the demand for it, resulting in prolonged bouts of unemployment or inflation. The process that ensues when such a disequilibrium appears is relatively well understood. If aggregate demand falls short of output, producers accumulate inventories and make losses. They borrow to keep afloat, but if the situation persists, they can no longer repay. The value of their shares which they may have used as collateral melts away—so that their bankruptcy infects their creditors, who must call in their loans to other industries in order to survive. Thus, financial contagion spreads far and wide. Meanwhile, the contracting firms lay off workers and stop investing in reducing demand even further. This is the vicious spiral of cumulative contraction. On the other hand, if demand outstrips output, producers accelerate orders and compete for labour and inputs, driving up wages and input prices even as they raise their own product prices. Share prices escalate, so do land and property prices in an upward race that is intensified by rising expectations into a speculative bubble. What initiates these cumulative processes and how they end or are reversed are more difficult questions. In the light of the general theme of this book, the market, if it is to do its job of coordination properly, must ensure that the output generated at full employment is just absorbed by demand so that neither depression nor inflation occurs. This objective is often not achieved in reality. Why isn't it?

Fig. 9.1

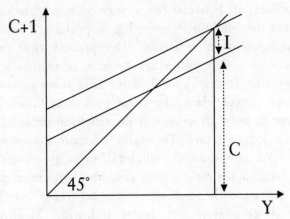

THE KEYNESIAN UNDEREMPLOYMENT EQUILIBRIUM

Keynes,[31] who, in *The General Theory of Employment, Interest and Money*, sought an answer to this question in the middle of the greatest crisis that modern capitalism has ever faced—the Great Depression of 1929–39—used, as his main analytical tool, the *consumption function*. He claimed that consumption C is related to income Y: an increase in income by a rupee raises consumption by a fraction of a rupee. This fraction he described as the *marginal propensity to consume*, c. While consumption spending increases with income, the other component of expenditure, investment I, is determined by long-term profit prospects and so is essentially independent of income. Total expenditure C + I represents the demand for the aggregate output of firms. In equilibrium, this must just equal the total cost

---

[31] J.M. Keynes, *The General Theory of Employment, Interest and Money* (London: Macmillan, 1936).

of firms, which is represented by the total income Y that they pay out to the factors of production they employ. Thus, the condition for equilibrium is C(Y) + I = Y where C(Y) represents consumption as a function of income. This condition is depicted in Fig. 9.1.

Equilibrium is reached at the point of intersection of the C(Y) + I line with the 45° line. Here, C(Y) + I = Y. So, here, all that households earn as income Y is exactly returned to the circular flow of income in the form of consumption or investment spending, so that this circular flow is maintained at a constant level. If C + I exceeds Y, income expands. So does consumption (but by a smaller amount since c < 1), thus narrowing the gap between expenditure and income. This process continues till the gap disappears altogether—and equilibrium is reached. Similarly, if Y exceeds C + I, income contracts till equilibrium is reached. An alternative statement of the same condition is I = Y − C(Y) = S(Y) where S(Y) represents savings as a function of income—income changes due to a discrepancy between desired savings and investment.

One way of understanding this process is to trace the path of a rupee spent as investment. The recipient of this rupee increases consumption by c; one person's expenditure of c becomes someone else's income and induces further consumption of c^2 and so on in a chain of successive re-spendings. The total income generated by the initial investment of a rupee is the infinite series:

$$M = 1 + c + c^2 + c^3 + c^4 + \ldots$$

A simple trick of high school algebra gives us a precise value for M. Multiply M by c and subtract the product cM from M:

$$cM = c + c^2 + c^3 + c^4 + \ldots$$
$$\text{So } M(1-c) = 1$$
$$\text{And } M = 1/(1 - c).$$

The expression $1/(1-c)$ is known as the multiplier, and indicates that any spending has a magnified effect on total income through the chain reaction of successive re-spendings that it sets off. The multiplier applies to any element of expenditure that is autonomous (independent of income): aggregate income is $M(I + A)$ where I is investment and A other autonomous expenditure.

Keynes argued that there was no reason why the equilibrium output thus determined would be the output produced by a fully employed workforce. It could be lower, in which case there would be persistent unemployment in equilibrium. It could be higher, leading to persistent inflation.

An implication of the Keynesian model of income determination is the *paradox of thrift*. If people wish to save more, if they reduce their propensity to consume c (increase their propensity to save, $s = 1 - c$), they will be unable to add to their total savings: as the propensity to save rises, the multiplier falls proportionally. Aggregate income falls in exact proportion to the rise in s, so that total savings remain unchanged. The presumption that a heightened desire to save results in higher aggregate savings has been described by Keynes as an example of the fallacy of composition: the belief that what is true for the part is necessarily true for the whole. If I save a rupee more, I inject a rupee less into the stream of expenditure and income. This not only reduces income directly by a rupee but also indirectly through the multiplier via its negative effects on successive re-spendings. Total income falls by $1/s$ (the multiplier) rupees. This reduces the savings of others by s. $1/s = 1$, i.e. by the one rupee by which I had increased my savings. Total savings remain entirely unaffected. In the Keynesian world, total savings are entirely determined in equilibrium by autonomous expenditure, regardless of the traditional virtues of prudence and thrift. As Mae West would have asserted: goodness had nothing to do with it, dearie!

In fact, the Keynesian ethic was the mirror image of the traditional. Keynes would most certainly have slaughtered the fatted calf to welcome the prodigal son because in the depressed world he lived in, it was the spendthrift who added to the multiplier and therefore to national income. Not that the prodigal sons of today need derive much comfort from the fact. In our inflationary times, he would no doubt have counselled them to rein in their spending in the interests of society, if not in their own interest.

KEYNES VERSUS THE CLASSICISTS

Keynes's *general theory* did much more than reverse the accepted canon of social behaviour. The Keynesian Revolution shook the very foundations of preexisting macro-economic theory by its insistence on the possibility of an equilibrium in which many millions of people were involuntarily unemployed, an equilibrium reached through a process of income and output contraction which was Keynes's main adjustment mechanism. The entire Classical tradition in economics from Adam Smith and J.B. Say[32] in the eighteenth century to A.C. Pigou[33] and Irving Fisher in the twentieth denied the possibility of such an equilibrium. It asserted that mass unemployment could

---

[32] J.B. Say, *A Treatise on Political Economy*, trans. C.R. Prinsep (Philadelphia: Grigg & Elliot, 1834).

[33] A.C. Pigou, 'The Classical Stationary State', *Economic Journal* 53 (1943): 343–51.

only be a disequilibrium, a temporary and self-limiting malady. The Classicists claimed that market disequilibria, like involuntary unemployment, induce price-, wage- and interest-rate changes that restore full-employment equilibrium. According to them, a threefold process ensures this outcome:

1. First, unemployed labour will be willing to work for lower wages and will be hired accordingly.
2. Second, when savings exceed investment, the supply of loans exceeds demand, driving down the interest rate, thus reducing the incentive to save and stimulating the incentive to invest, thereby reducing the saving–investment gap eventually to zero.
3. Third, when demand for goods falls short of supply, the immediate impact (before production and employment are curtailed) is a fall in prices. The fall in prices increases the real purchasing power of the cash balances held by people, inducing them to demand more goods, thus narrowing the supply–demand gap.

The Keynesians, on the other hand, argued that these adjustment processes were aborted by rigidities of factor and commodity prices which perpetuated disequilibrium:

1. Wages are not reduced even when unemployed workers offer to work for less than the market rate because *employers* do not regard wage cuts to be in their interest: (a) the wage represents the value of the job to the worker and so determines how eager he is to work in order to minimize the risk of dismissal if caught shirking by the employer in the course of a random check; (b) the wage that the employee offers to work for represents the

employee's own assessment of his ability—so if he offers to work for a low wage, that signals to the employer the fact that his productivity is low; (c) a worker who gets his job by offering to work for a lower wage risks the resentment of his colleagues who may then deny him their cooperation, thus reducing productivity in any teamwork situation.[34]

2. Interest rates cannot fall below the *liquidity trap* level, the level below which the rate of return on loans is too low to compensate for the risks (of capital loss through depreciation or default) and administrative costs of lending.

3. Commodity prices are kept up by unions and oligopolistic firms that prefer to reduce output when business is bad rather than to cut prices (since that might precipitate a price war with their rivals).

WAGE RIGIDITY

Let us spell out a few of these arguments in some detail. The rigidity of wages stems largely from asymmetric information between the employer and the employee. The employer has no clue as to whether his employee is busy with work or with tea and gossip except through expensive vigilance round the clock. His best option is to organize random surprise checks and to instantly dismiss anyone found shirking. Of course, if dismissal from one job merely opens the door to another at the same wage (as it might if the economy is at full employment), dismissal will be an empty threat which deters

---

[34] Carl Shapiro and Joseph Stiglitz, 'Equilibrium Unemployment as a Worker Discipline Device', *The American Economic Review* 74 (1984): 433–44.

no one. Therefore, the employer must reinforce his threat by paying higher-than-market wages. But if all employers try to do this, the market wage itself will be driven above the full-employment market-clearing level by competitive wage offers. As wages rise, employers can no longer afford to hire as many as before. They will have to restrict employment in order to prevent the marginal product of labour falling below the wage they offer. Involuntary unemployment will emerge, and it will be the increased risk of joblessness that will now lend a sharp edge to the threat of dismissal. Unemployment, rather than the prospect of a lower wage, will be the worker-disciplining device of the economy.

This is wage rigidity designed by the employer to deter shirking. It focuses on averting moral hazard induced by the employer's inability to continuously monitor the actions of the employee. There is also, however, an adverse selection aspect of the employer–employee relationship that rears its ugly head at the hiring stage itself. The employer doesn't really know the quality of the worker he is hiring—certainly not as well as the worker himself. It is the worker who best knows what the market value of his services is, and he will certainly not accept a wage lower than this. The lower the wage that the employer sets, the lower the quality of the workers he attracts and, beyond a point, he will therefore not be willing to reduce his wage offer any further.

Asymmetric information supplies two of the main causes of wage rigidity. A third cause is what has sometimes been described as the 'insider–outsider' problem. Incumbent workers have a mutual loyalty which induces hostility to any newcomer who displaces one of them by offering to work for a lower wage. Even if he doesn't replace any one, his addition to the labour force itself provokes resentment.

If an outsider can join at a lower wage, who knows when some insiders will be dispensed with in favour of cheaper recruits? Insider morale is undermined and teamwork suffers as insiders deny their cooperation to the outsider.

THE LIQUIDITY TRAP

The liquidity trap is a component of the Keynesian theory of money. It has long been recognized that money is indispensable for the growth of trade beyond basic barter. In a barter economy, I can trade only with someone who needs what I have a surplus of and who can offer me what I need. Trade is based on this double coincidence of wants. If, however, a social convention evolves that a particular object, reasonably abundant and possibly of no intrinsic value, is generally acceptable as money, the tyranny of double coincidence is overthrown. I can sell to anyone who wants what I have, earn money and spend it on buying what I want from somebody altogether different. Money becomes the prime facilitator of almost all economic transactions as a *medium of exchange* and the demand for money as an exchange medium is therefore a function of the volume of transactions (therefore of the level of output). However, typically money is durable; it can be used to store and transfer value from a particular place or time to another. And this *store-of-value* function of money is the source of much heartburn. When money is held as a store of value, one misses out on an earning opportunity which can be regarded as the price of money, the interest that could have been earned by lending it out. What is more, this loan is typically given in return for a bond, a promise to pay not only the interest but also the principal at a fixed future date. Meanwhile, the bond can be traded in the market and its value can fluctuate; people can speculate on it and win a fortune or lose their all and commit suicide. There is, therefore, a speculative demand for money, which is inversely related to the rate of interest. The lower the interest rate, the cheaper it is to hold money. Also, the lower the interest rate, the likelier it is that it will rise in future, so that profitable lending opportunities will expand with time. There would be an interest rate so low that no one would want to lend today. The return from doing so would simply not offset the risks and costs of doing so, one of which would be not having cash on hand when lending becomes worthwhile again. At this rate, all financial assets are held as idle cash, the interest rate cannot sink any further and ceases to function as an equilibrating mechanism.

PRICE RIGIDITY

The standard context of price rigidity is oligopolistic concern about the reactions of one's rivals, as described by the Marxian economist Paul Sweezy.[35] One avoids raising prices lest one's competitors, instead of doing the good-neighbourly thing of following suit, persist with their old prices in the hope of luring away one's clientele. One avoids lowering prices too because of the suspicion that one's competitors, instead of meekly letting their migrants shift loyalties, will match any price cut. Such suspicions are strongly reinforced when excess capacity prevails industry-wide, as is likely during a depression. Demand fluctuations affect output, not prices.

---

[35] Paul Sweezy, 'Demand Under Conditions of Oligopoly', *The Journal of Political Economy* 47 (1939): 568–73.

This has two implications. First, as indicated above, prices are especially rigid during depressions due to the presence of excess capacity. During booms, they operate at full capacity and have little interest in snatching away the customers of a rival who has raised prices: they are likely therefore to follow any price increase. Prices therefore respond asymmetrically to booms and busts. They are likelier to rise in boom-time than to fall during recessions. This contributes to a worldwide secular inflationary trend.

Secondly, prices are more rigid in oligopolistic activities like large-scale manufacturing than in competitive sectors like agriculture. Depressions, therefore, produce dramatic collapses in agricultural prices. Industry, on the other hand, is characterized by large-scale unemployment rather than downward price spirals.

An important exception to oligopolistic price rigidity is the situation described in the last section of Chapter 7, where the oligopolists charge the monopoly price and share the monopoly profit in equilibrium. Here, as industry demand contracts, the monopoly price falls; the oligopolists will then cut prices accordingly, tempering the reduction in output.

Whatever the precise mechanisms and exceptions—and there are many that we have not mentioned—the Keynesian and Classical schools of thought disagree largely because of their differing perceptions of the degree of flexibility of the price system.

JOB SEARCH

A question of some importance: if the Classicists deny the possibility of long-term involuntary unemployment, how do they explain the observed persistence for many years of large volumes of unemployment? The answer relates to the process of job search. Job hunting is costly and the returns to it depend on the difference between the wage that the job promises and the income—both monetary and psychic—enjoyed by the jobless. There is hence a minimum wage below which job search ceases. This threshold depends on the income of the jobless. The higher the latter, the less inclined will the unemployed be to search for jobs. Therefore, social devices like unemployment compensation increase the level of visible unemployment by discouraging job search. However, this unemployment is *voluntary*.

THE CLASSICAL CRITIQUE OF THE CONSUMPTION FUNCTION

The Classicists also reject the Keynesian theory of the consumption function and the related model of the multiplier. They argue that our consumption needs are relatively stable while our income either changes sharply over our lifecycle or is highly volatile, so that people plan their consumption not on the basis of their current income, but of their long-term income prospects:

1. Chicago economist Milton Friedman[36] argued that consumption is linked to average expected long-term income (*permanent income*) and responds to current income changes only to the extent that they affect long-term income prospects.

---

[36] Milton Friedman, *A Theory of the Consumption Function* (Princeton: Princeton University Press, 1957).

2. Franco Modigliani[37] of the Massachusetts Institute of
    Technology (MIT) claimed that consumption and income
    follow a regular pattern over our *lifecycles*: (a) early
    in our working lives, our income may fall short of our
    consumption requirements, forcing us to borrow; (b) as
    our income rises to a peak in mid-career, we can repay our
    loans and save for our old age; and (c) after retirement, our
    income falls and we must live on our accumulated savings.

Both these theories imply that consumption is not very
responsive to current income. Empirical evidence suggests,
however, an *excess sensitivity* of consumption to current
income over what the permanent income or lifecycle
hypotheses predict. This excess sensitivity probably reflects
the fact that credit constraints (due to moral hazard—
lenders are not sure that they will be repaid) prevent people
with temporarily low incomes from borrowing as much as is
warranted by their long-term income prospects.

Apart from income, whether in the long run or the short,
and consumer preferences, there are two other factors that
affect consumption. First, the consumer's budget includes
not only his income but his liquid assets as well. Of these,
the non-cash financial assets are matched by the liabilities
of other people in the economy and therefore cancel out
in the process of aggregation over the entire population.
But that still leaves the cash. The purchasing power of cash
balances affects the budget constraint and therefore all

---

[37] Franco Modigliani and Richard Brumberg, 'Utility Analysis and
the Consumption Function', in *Post-Keynesian Economics,* ed.
K. Kurihara (New Brunswick, NJ: Rutgers University Press,
1954), pp. 338–46.

consumption decisions. As the price level rises, the real value of these balances melts away and so consumption declines: a phenomenon described as the Pigou–Patinkin effect after its main proponents, A.C. Pigou of Cambridge and Don Patinkin[38] of the Hebrew University, Jerusalem. Second, the interest rate enters into our consumption decisions as the price of current consumption, a fact emphasized in Chapter 4. Generally, though not always, this implies that consumption falls as the interest rate rises.

KEYNES AND THE CLASSICS ON MACRO-ECONOMIC POLICY

What do these two rival schools of thought prescribe in terms of macro-economic policy? The Keynesians believe that unemployment can be controlled by *fiscal expansion*: increased government spending and reduced taxes (possibly entailing a deficit budget). Both measures put more income in the hands of people. Through its multiplier effects, this has a magnified impact on aggregate income and employment. In contrast, they regard monetary policy—expansion of the money supply—to be ineffective since it cannot drive down the price of money and the interest rate (and so stimulate spending) if we are in the liquidity trap, as we are likely to be in deep depressions. Similarly, inflation can be controlled by fiscal contraction, though monetary policy is more effective here than in recessions since there is no upper limit to the interest rate (unlike the lower limit set by the liquidity trap).

---

[38] Don Patinkin, *Money, Interest and Prices: An Integration of Monetary and Value Theory* (Cambridge, MA: MIT Press, 1956).

The Classicists argue that fiscal policy is bound to be useless. Any increase in government spending, if not financed by higher taxes, must be funded by borrowing—the government competes with private borrowers for loans and drives up the interest rate, *crowding out* private borrowing and spending. There is, thus, no net increase in expenditure, just a replacement of private spending by government spending, especially since the multiplier effect is held to be a myth. Monetary policy may be more effective in stimulating expenditure by reducing interest rates. However, the main policy instrument should be encouragement to job search, notably by cutting unemployment benefits. Inflation control, likewise, is best accomplished by reducing the money supply.

To clarify things further, let's examine fiscal policy in depressions first from the Keynesian and then from the Classical viewpoint. In the Keynesian model, government expenditure adds to demand, both directly and through its multiplier effects on consumer spending. In response to higher demand, producers expand production by hiring more labour and investing in more machinery. The investments may be financed by borrowing. These increases in output are achieved without significant rise in unit cost since labour is available in highly elastic supply at the ruling wage and loans at the current interest rate. Thus, employment and output expand at unchanged prices.

The Classicists deny the possibility of an infinitely elastic supply of loans at the liquidity trap rate even in a depression. They argue, therefore, that government spending adds very little to demand: it mostly crowds out private investment through higher interest rates and has no multiplier effects (since the Keynesian consumption function does not exist). The small increase in aggregate demand is dissipated in rising wages and prices; it does not yield increase in output.

In contrast to their enthusiasm about fiscal policy, Keynesians are very negative about monetary policy. In a depression, they believe an increase in money supply will be absorbed in idle cash balances; it cannot drive the interest rate below the liquidity trap level. So it cannot find its way into circulation and cannot therefore affect the real economy. On the other hand, the Classicists believe that monetary expansion will depress interest rates temporarily and stimulate spending. But since there is no involuntary unemployment, competition for labour drives up wages and prices; when prices have risen in proportion to the money supply, all real variables return to their old values.

The purchasing power of money reverts to what it was before the increase in money supply, aggregate demand in real terms is restored to its old level and we converge on an equilibrium in which prices are precisely proportional to money supply. This is a modern restatement of the older doctrine known as the quantity theory of money—in long-run equilibrium, money affects prices alone but no real variables. Behind the veil of money, the real economy functions quite independently.

RICARDIAN EQUIVALENCE AND THE NEUTRALITY OF THE PUBLIC DEBT

A policy issue of some importance relates to the role of budget deficits. When the budget is balanced, government spending returns to the private income stream exactly what it withdraws in taxes; private income and demand therefore remain what they were while the government's expenditure adds an equivalent sum to aggregate demand. The *balanced budget multiplier* is just 1. A budget deficit, however, implies that expenditure is matched not by taxes but by borrowing; not only are the borrowings returned to the private sector through government expenditure, but wealth in the form of government bonds is created and left in the hands of private individuals. Keynesians may argue that this added wealth encourages the bondholders to spend more, thus magnifying the demand effect of government expenditure. However, government bonds are not just assets; they are liabilities as well, since they have to be serviced and repaid. If today's bondholders and tomorrow's taxpayers are the same individuals, no *net* wealth is created and public debt is therefore *neutral* in its impact on demand. This is the essence of a notion pioneered by the nineteenth-century economist David Ricardo[39] and rediscovered and described by Harvard economist Robert Barro[40]—tax finance and debt finance are essentially equivalent in their effects on aggregate spending.

Public debt, of course, has to be repaid only in the fairly distant future. So, if I discount the interests of posterity heavily, the repayment obligations will sit too lightly on my mind to deter my present extravagances. Ricardian equivalence will hold strictly only for a generation that sees

---

[39] David Ricardo, 'Essay on the Funding System', in *The Works of David Ricardo*, ed. J.R. McCulloch (London: John Murray, 1888).

[40] Robert Barro, 'Are Government Bonds Net Wealth?', *Journal of Political Economy* 82 (1974): 1095–117.

itself living into the indefinite future through the lives of its descendants.

THE PHILLIPS CURVE AND RATIONAL EXPECTATIONS

In the 1940s and 1950s, observers noticed that there appeared to be a policy trade-off between unemployment and inflation. Governments could generally reduce unemployment, but only at the cost of higher inflation. The negative relationship between the rate of unemployment and that of inflation was called the *Phillips Curve*.[41] Governments tried to exploit this by selecting their preferred combination of unemployment and inflation on this curve. From the 1970s, however, the Phillips curve suddenly vanished. *Stagflation*, the coexistence of unemployment and output stagnation with high inflation, became endemic.

What explained the appearance and sudden disappearance of the Phillips Curve? When the price of a product rises, the producer finds it profitable to expand output and employment if he does not expect wages and other input prices also to rise. However, if all producers are doing the same, this will inevitably drive wages and other prices up and the higher rate of employment and output can be sustained only by a further rise in price. Thus, a given employment (or unemployment) rate becomes associated with a particular rate of price rise, as long as people do not

---

[41] A.W. Phillips, 'The Relationship between Unemployment and the Rate of Change of Money Wages in the United Kingdom 1861–1957', *Economica* 25 (1958): 283–99.

expect this price rise to become general. However, after several experiences, people learn to expect general inflation (and a consequent rise in their costs) when they see the price of their product rising; they no longer consider it profitable to expand output and employment. Inflation no longer yields a dividend in terms of employment growth and the Phillips Curve disappears.

A substantially modified version of the Phillips Curve still survives in macro-economic theory. If the actual rate of inflation exceeds the anticipated rate, the employment-increasing effects described above will occur—as long as expectations do not catch up with reality. Thus, an *expectations-augmented Phillips Curve* reappears, but with a short lease of life. It certainly cannot serve as a policy instrument in the long run.

The will-o'-the-wisp behaviour of the Phillips Curve led to the development of the theory of *rational expectations* by Robert Lucas[42] and Thomas Sargent.[43] This theory postulates that in the long run, people's expectations never depart *systematically* from reality. Therefore, any effort by the government to induce an error in expectations on the part of private citizens is bound to fail in the long run. In the 1970s, the US government repeatedly sought to stimulate the economy by mild inflation, but producers rapidly adjusted their inflation expectations upward and did not therefore expand employment and output. Government can take the

[42] Robert Lucas, 'Expectations and the Neutrality of Money', *Journal of Economic Theory* 4 (1972): 103–24.
[43] Thomas Sargent and Neil Wallace, '"Rational" Expectations, the Optimal Monetary Instrument, and the Optimal Money Supply Rule', *Journal of Political Economy* 83 (1975): 241–54.

citizenry by surprise only by occasional accident, certainly not as a general rule. In general, this theory underlines policy ineffectiveness—the impotence of government when it seeks to change popular expectations in the long run. The policy ineffectiveness proposition is not of course universally accepted. It has been argued that in order to form rational expectations, individuals need to inform themselves at much expense of time and money. But their actions will reveal their information to their competitors, so that they will be unable to benefit from the information they have acquired. Why then would they acquire the information? Further, even if they do and rationally expect prices to rise, say, on the basis of the information they have collected, they may be constrained from demanding higher wages by long-term wage contracts they may have signed. Meanwhile, in the immediate present, real wages can fall, and labour demand, employment and output can increase as the policymakers had planned.

In a wider perspective, macro-economic policy can be understood as part of a sequential game between the private sector and the government in which the expectations of one about the actions of the other, not just today but in future as well, are crucial. The government may make the first move, to which individuals and firms react and the government then has the chance to modify its initial step. If the government can commit itself *credibly* to a long-term policy, the private sector must accept this as a given parameter; it cannot manipulate the future course of government policy through its own actions. Credible commitment, however, requires a surrender of discretion by the government. If it retains the option of flexible response, this creates the problem of *dynamic inconsistency.*[44] At the second stage, once the private sector's reaction is an accomplished fact, the government may find it worthwhile to renege on its pre-announced policy; but if it does so, no one will believe its commitments in future. The subgame-perfect Nash equilibrium of this game may not be compatible with the pre-announced promise (or threat). The private sector knows this of course, and its initial reaction takes this into account so that the government's policies and announcements never have the desired effect. A strong case is thus made out for government to follow well-defined and rigid rules that are legally or constitutionally prescribed rather than discretionary policy.

SUMMARY

Macro-economics is the economics of aggregates. It explores the question of how variables like national income and output, the volume of employment and the general level of prices are determined. Modern macro-economics originated in Keynes's abandonment of traditional thinking in the middle of the Great Depression of 1929–39. He argued that national income was determined at the point where the savings that people withdrew from the circular flow of income (and which he believed to be monotonically related to current income) were precisely returned to the income stream in the form of investment expenditure. Given the level of investment, national income

---

[44] Finn Kydland and Edward Prescott, 'Rules Rather than Discretion: The Inconsistency of Optimal Plans', *Journal of Political Economy* (1977): 473–92.

formation could be visualized as the process of successive consumption re-spending of the income directly generated by the investment. This multiplied the income effect of the initial investment by a factor that depended on the marginal propensity to consume. It was infinitely improbable that income in the Keynesian equilibrium would be what a fully employed labour force would produce.

Keynesian analysis was strongly disputed by the Classicists. They argued that if savings out of full-employment income exceeded investment, three other adjustment processes would be set off that would restore equilibrium without income having to contract:

1. Interest rates would be driven down, stimulating both consumption and investment.
2. Prices would fall, increasing the purchasing power of the cash held by people and inducing them to spend.
3. Wages would decline, encouraging employers to hire more labour.

The Keynesians countered that downward rigidities of interest rates, wages and prices would abort these processes, leaving income contraction as the only mechanism of adjustment. If investment exceeded saving, these processes could work better since there were no upward rigidities and since output could not increase once the full employment ceiling had been reached.

The policy recommendations of the rival schools reflected their theoretical positions. Keynesians favoured fiscal policy in depressions—increased government spending and tax cuts, financed if necessary by borrowing. Classicists claimed that fiscal policy was useless; all it could do was to crowd out private spending through the rise in interest rates induced by public borrowing. Keynesians asserted that monetary policy was ineffectual; a higher money supply would simply be absorbed into idle cash hoards. Classicists believed that monetary expansion in depressions would temporarily drive down interest rates and stimulate spending, but that this would raise prices, erode the real value of cash balances down to what they were earlier and restore real demand to its earlier value. The Classicists regarded prolonged unemployment as essentially voluntary: the product of reduced job search due to the cushion provided by unemployment compensation. The long-run solution to such unemployment was a cut in unemployment benefits.

An issue of some interest in this context revolved around the financing of deficits. Should we close the deficit by taxation or borrow the necessary amount? Keynesians believed that through public debt, we could pass on our obligations to posterity. However, if we also happen to pass on bequests, the value of any asset that we may bequeath is reduced by the taxes that would have to be paid to service the public debt. In order to make a bequest of the same value as before, we would have to set aside more savings; while passing on our obligations to future generations, we also pass on the means of fulfilling them. Public debt is neutral in its impact on our wealth and therefore on our expenditures.

An empirical phenomenon of the 1950s and 1960s was the Phillips Curve, an apparent trade-off between higher inflation and higher unemployment which macro-economic data seemed to reveal. However, when policymakers sought to exploit this relationship, it suddenly vanished. A higher inflation target, once the policymakers set their sights on it, became generally anticipated—and failed, thereafter, to reduce the degree of unemployment. This experience led to the rational expectations hypothesis that asserted that people's expectations would never be systematically wrong. Policymakers cannot deliberately sustain an illusion for any length of time.

A second related policy issue is that of credibility. Governments that retain policy discretion cannot credibly announce any long-term policy: the private sector knows that after it has reacted to the initial announcement, it may be optimal for the government to deviate from the pre-announced policy. It is only a government that has legally or constitutionally committed itself to a fixed rule that will be believed and will therefore be able to implement a policy in the long run.

PROBLEM

1. Suppose the government of Illyria commits itself to providing 100 days of employment annually digging ditches and filling them up to any individual on demand. The money wage offered is predetermined and reasonable. The scheme is financed entirely by additional taxation. What will happen to output, employment and prices?

Chapter 10

International Trade Theory

We have focused up to this point on a closed economy. The planet as a whole is indeed a closed system and is likely to remain so at least as long as space travel remains largely confined to the realms of science fiction. Even so, however, the reality of national borders and sovereignties divides up the world economy into fragments that are only very imperfectly unified. Restrictions on the movement of goods and factors across boundaries are major determinants of what goes on in any national economy; international income inequalities can in large measure be explained by them. Transport costs also divide up the world economy, but the differences they create are interregional (between separate geographical areas) rather than international (between separate countries).

International trade theory is essentially concerned with the economic consequences of restrictions on the flow of people, goods and capital across national frontiers.

Its starting point is a hypothetical world of free trade in commodities, but with all factors of production bound to their roots by migration restrictions. This, of course, is only a yardstick, against which alternative regimes of international trade can be measured. But it is a model of great interest and influence and one that has shaped the thinking of economists and politicians the world over.

CAUSES OF INTERNATIONAL TRADE

Why in a world that permits free trade should there be any trade at all? Economists distinguish two major causes of trade:

1. Economies of scale: The first of these, elaborated by Adam Smith[45] in *The Wealth of Nations*, is summarized famously by his maxim, 'The division of labour is limited by the size of the market.' Any increase in the area of trade enables the traders to specialize in particular fields of production (and so exploit economies of large scale) instead of each having to produce all his requirements. It doesn't matter which field each specializes in or whether the traders differ in the structure of their productive abilities. All that matters is the fact of division of labour.
2. Comparative advantage: The second prime cause of trade, emphasized by Smith's great successor Ricardo,[46] greatly magnified the effect of the first—where the traders differ in the structure of their productive

---

[45] Smith, *Wealth of Nations*.
[46] David Ricardo, *On the Principles of Political Economy and Taxation* (London: John Murray, 1817).

abilities, trade enables each to concentrate on what he does best. Function is thereby adapted to capacity, production pattern to endowments. Most subsequent theory focused on comparative advantage, ruling out the Smithian basis for trade by assuming constant returns to scale (CRS). Note that Ricardo is talking about *comparative*, rather than absolute, advantage: if the world's best economist is also the world's best cook (but by a narrower margin), he would benefit by hiring a cook who is somewhat worse than him and using the time thus saved on writing economics papers.

SOURCES OF COMPARATIVE ADVANTAGE: THE FACTOR ENDOWMENTS THEORY

The main source of comparative advantage (i.e. of differences in the structure of productive abilities between different trading countries) is difference in their resource endowments. Countries that are relatively capital-abundant (having a higher proportion of capital to labour) have a comparative advantage in producing capital-intensive goods (such as sophisticated machinery) while labour-abundant countries have a comparative advantage in labour-intensive production (such as garments and shoes). To understand this, assume the contrary. Suppose that a capital-abundant and a labour-abundant country produce both goods in the same proportion when both sell at the same relative price in the two countries. They will then be using the two factors in the same proportion as well, but their endowments differ. The capital-abundant country will therefore have a surplus of capital and the labour-abundant country a surplus of labour. This will lead to a fall in the price of capital and consequently in the unit cost of the capital-intensive good in the capital-abundant country. It will also depress the price of labour and the unit cost of the labour-intensive good in the labour-abundant country. Given the same commodity-price ratio, producers in each country will switch to producing more of the lower unit cost good: more of the capital-intensive good in the capital-rich country and more of the labour-intensive good in the labour-rich country. Thus, the composition of output in the two countries will reflect their relative factor endowments. Unless this pattern of comparative advantage in production is offset by a similar bias in consumption (i.e. capital-abundant countries also consuming a higher proportion of capital-intensive goods and vice versa for labour-abundant countries), it will be reflected in their trade pattern: capital-abundant countries will not only produce more capital-intensive goods but also export them while importing labour-intensive products. This is the factor endowments theory of international trade developed by the Swedish economists Eli Heckscher and Bertil Ohlin.[47]

COROLLARIES OF THE FACTOR ENDOWMENTS THEORY

Factor-Price Equalization

The Heckscher–Ohlin theory was the centrepiece of a series of theoretical developments by Paul Samuelson and others that created the modern theory of international trade.

---

[47] Bertil Ohlin, *Interregional and International Trade* (Cambridge, MA: Harvard University Press, 1933).

Possibly the most important of these was the factor-price equalization (FPE) theorem.[48]

Samuelson showed in FPE that a small set of fairly innocuous sounding assumptions sufficed to ensure that free trade in commodities could in most cases be a perfect substitute for free factor movement: uniform world prices for goods would generally guarantee equality of factor prices worldwide despite the persistence of migration restrictions. FPE thus provided a major rationale for global free trade.

Stripped down to its essentials, FPE required only five assumptions:

1. Perfect mobility of goods.
2. Identical technologies.
3. Perfect competition.
4. CRS.
5. Perfect international immobility of factors.

If goods are perfectly mobile, a uniform price will rule worldwide for each good. For any pair of goods, a uniform price ratio will prevail in every country where both goods are produced. The assumption of identical technologies worldwide was based on the belief that in the long run, technological knowledge is freely available (note that there was no assumption of identical *techniques*—the actual methods of production, the capital/labour ratios were endogenously determined). The perfect competition assumption meant that, as in long-run competitive equilibrium, the price of each good equals its unit cost. So, a uniform price ratio implies

---

[48] Paul Samuelson, 'International Trade and the Equalisation of Factor Prices', *Economic Journal* (1948): 163–84.

a uniform ratio of unit costs. Under CRS, unit costs are independent of the scale of production—they depend only on factor prices. The assumption of perfect international immobility of factors was added to ensure that the result of the theorem owed nothing to international factor migration.

Now, under CRS, as we have seen in Chapter 5 (Fig. 5.2), factor proportions in each industry are determined by the wage/rental ratio. As wage, w, rises relative to the rental, r, on capital, the cheaper factor is substituted for the dearer, and the labour/capital ratio falls. The relationship is depicted in the first quadrant of Fig. 10.1 by downward-sloping *factor-intensity curves*. Each industry is characterized by its own distinctive factor-intensity curve. Fig. 10.1 portrays a situation in which the factor-intensity curve of industry X lies everywhere to the right of that of industry Y. This implies that industry X is more labour-intensive than industry Y at all wage-rental ratios: a property known as *strong factor intensity*.

Fig. 10.1: Strong Factor Intensity

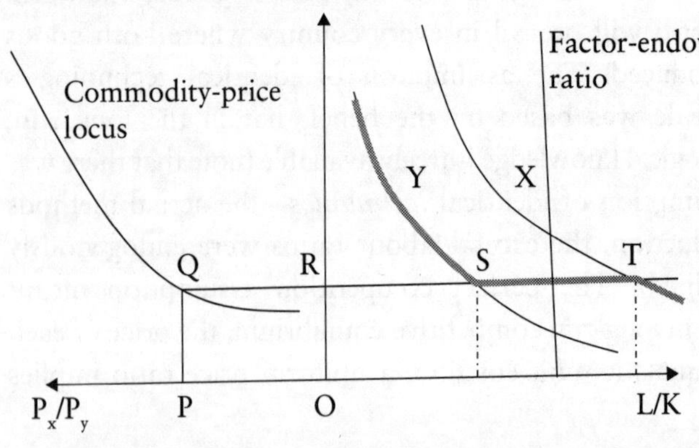

The second quadrant of Fig. 10.1 displays the *commodity price locus*: the relationship between the ratio of commodity prices p_x/p_y and the wage-rental ratio w/r. In all industries that survive in long-run competitive equilibrium, commodity prices converge to the respective unit costs and since X is always more labour-intensive than Y, a rise in the wage-rental ratio always raises the unit cost (and therefore the price) of X relative to that of Y. The commodity price locus is monotonically upward sloping.

Fig. 10.1 is constructed purely on the basis of the technological characteristics of industries X and Y. It does not use any information about factor endowments or any other country-specific characteristics. It is, therefore, valid for all countries that share the same technologies, and by assumption, all do.

The figure indicates that at any commodity-price ratio (say OP), there will be a unique factor-price ratio (OR) in any country where both X and Y are produced. In all such countries, free trade will, by ensuring uniform commodity prices, equalize factor prices, regardless of their factor endowments.

But the figure does more than that. It indicates the circumstances under which both goods will be produced and, therefore, factor prices will be equalized. It also tells us what will happen if factor prices are not equalized.

Suppose the world commodity-price ratio is OP, implying a factor-price ratio OR: industries X and Y will use labour and capital in the ratios RT and RS, respectively. The ratio in which factors are demanded in aggregate will be an average of RT and RS and must therefore lie between them. But then factor-market equilibrium requires that the supply of factors (the factor endowment) must also lie between these limits as illustrated in Fig. 10.1. These limits define a zone of diversification or imperfect specialization within which both industries operate. The precise value of the factor-endowment ratio determines the shares of each industry in the total employment of the inputs. If L/K increases, the factor-endowment line shifts to the right closer to the factor-intensity curve of the labour-intensive X industry, implying that the share of the labour-intensive industry in factor employment rises. If the factor endowment lies outside the zone of diversification, say, L/K exceeds RT, not only will there be complete specialization in the labour-intensive industry but there will also be a surplus of labour and a shortage of capital at the wage-rental ratio OR; the wage will be driven up and the rental of capital driven down till the entire factor endowment can be absorbed in the labour-intensive industry X. Equilibrium will occur on the down-sloping segment of X's factor-intensity curve to the right of the diversification zone. If, on the other hand, L/K falls short of RS, equilibrium will be achieved on Y's factor-intensity curve to the left of the diversification zone. The locus of possible equilibria at different factor endowments consistent with the world commodity-price ratio OP is given by the three-stage bold curve in Fig. 10.1.

Fig. 10.2: Factor-Intensity Reversal

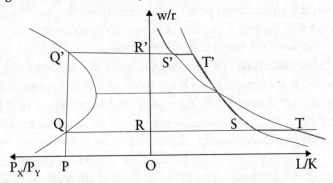

What if the strong factor-intensity property is violated? The factor-intensity curves will then intersect as in Fig. 10.2. At wage-rental ratios above the intersection, industry X is more labour-intensive and the commodity price locus is upward sloping as in Fig. 10.1. Below the intersection, the industries switch relative factor intensities. Industry Y has more flexible technology—it adapts better to falling w/r by adopting more labour-intensive techniques. At w/r below the intersection, since industry Y is now more labour-intensive, the commodity price locus will slope downward. The world commodity-price ratio OP is now associated, not with a unique factor-price ratio, but with multiple ratios—in the present example, with the two factor-price ratios OR and OR'. There will now be two diversification zones ST and S'T', corresponding to the two factor-price ratios and the three-stage bold curve of Fig. 10.1 is replaced by a five-stage bold curve with two horizontal segments and three down-sloping sections.

All this does not of course establish universal FPE through free commodity trade. It does, however, imply that free trade will have two consequences:

1. All countries with factor-endowment ratios within the limits of any particular horizontal segment would share the same factor-price ratio.
2. Where factor-price ratios are not equalized between a pair of countries, the country with the higher capital/labour ratio would have the higher wage/rental ratio.

THE RYBCZYNSKI THEOREM[49]

This theorem asserts that, if relative commodity prices are fixed (as, for instance, under free trade at world

---

[49] T.M. Rybczynski, 'Factor Endowment and Relative Commodity Prices', *Economica* 22 (1955): 336–41.

price levels), an increase in the quantity of one factor (say labour) would increase the quantity of the labour-intensive commodity and reduce that of the capital-intensive commodity. As the statement of the theorem makes evident, the implicit assumption is that both goods are being produced: we are in the diversification zone, at a point on ST in Fig.10.1. An increase in labour raises L/K; the factor-endowment ratio line shifts to the right; the proportion of each input employed in the capital-intensive Y industry falls. Since the total quantity of K in the economy has not changed, the absolute quantity used in producing Y must have fallen. But we are still at the old wage-rental ratio, using the old techniques of production at the old factor productivities. So a decline in one input in industry Y results in an absolute contraction in the output of Y. Since all inputs in industry X have increased, the output of X must increase.

THE STOLPER–SAMUELSON THEOREM

This is the symmetric dual of the Rybczynski theorem and can be obtained by interchanging the words 'factor' and 'commodity' and the words 'quantity' and 'price'. It states that if the factor endowments are fixed, an increase in the price of one commodity (for instance due to protection, say, of the capital-intensive good) would increase the price of the factor used intensively by it (say, capital) and reduce that of the other factor. Consider Fig. 10.3, adapted from the earlier Fig. 10.1. A factor-endowment ratio of OR is compatible with any commodity-price ratio between OP and OQ. But as the relative price of the labour-intensive good X rises from OP to OQ, the wage-rental ratio will rise

Fig. 10.3

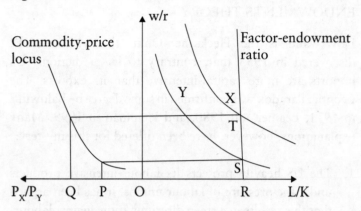

from RS to RT and the composition of output will change from complete specialization in the capital-intensive good Y to diversification to complete specialization in the labour-intensive good X. A higher wage-rental ratio cannot be sustained because that would result in unemployment of labour, driving w/r back down. Similarly, a wage-rental ratio below RS will result in unemployment of capital. However, the central message of Stolper and Samuelson[50] is that if the Heckscher–Ohlin result holds (countries are exporting goods intensive in their abundant factor and importing those intensive in their scarce factor), protection against imports would skew income distribution against their abundant factor and in favour of their scarce factor. In pre-reform India, the pervasive protection of imports (which were largely capital-intensive) meant higher profits and lower wages.

---

[50] Wolfgang Stolper and Paul Samuelson, 'Protection and real wages', *The Review of Economic Studies* 9 (1941): 58–73.

EMPIRICAL EVIDENCE ON THE FACTOR ENDOWMENTS THEORY

How valid is the Heckscher–Ohlin theory? Leontief[51] discovered in 1953 that, contrary to its predictions, US imports are more capital-intensive than its exports. The Leontief Paradox was confirmed in some degree by Baldwin[52] in 1971, Leamer[53] in 1980, and Helpman in 1999. Many explanations, however, have been offered for this mystery:

1. The US heavily protects its labour-intensive products under the pressure of labour unions. It has been argued that this results in a steep discrimination against labour-intensive imports which offsets the compulsions of factor endowment.
2. US labour is highly skilled due to heavy capital investment in its education. In fact, US labour should really be regarded as human capital and US exports are essentially human capital-intensive. They are hi-tech products that embody much R&D investment, for which 'labour' is a misnomer.
3. Leontief's dichotomy between capital and labour overlooks the crucial role of natural resources in US trade. US exports, which Leontief considers labour-intensive, are largely agricultural. US imports are largely

[51] Wassily Leontief, 'Domestic Production and Foreign Trade: The American Capital Position Re-examined', *Proceedings of the American Philosophical Society* 97 (1953): 332–49.
[52] Robert Baldwin, 'Determinants of the Commodity Structure of US Trade', *The American Economic Review* 61 (1971): 126–46.
[53] Edward Leamer, 'The Leontief Paradox, Reconsidered', *Journal of Political Economy* 88 (1980): 332–49.

minerals and replace or supplement domestic production that is highly capital-intensive. Thus Leontief, who did not take natural resources into account in his two-factor story, misinterpreted the US's vast agricultural exports as labour-intensive (when in fact they should have been classed as land-intensive in a more complete model). He also mislabelled the US's mineral imports as capital-intensive and concluded that the US had a comparative disadvantage in capital-intensive products when these imports simply reflected the fact that geography had not endowed the US with mineral resources adequate for her industrial needs.

Leontief's test therefore neither confirms nor refutes Heckscher–Ohlin.

More generally, however, if relative factor endowments determine production and export patterns, one would expect thinly populated countries to produce and export agricultural and other land-intensive products (minerals, etc.), while densely populated countries produce and export manufactures and services. Among manufactures, the capital-intensive ones (such as aircraft, precision tools, high-quality electronic, medical or optical equipment) are likelier to be produced and exported by wealthy capital-abundant countries while densely populated labour-abundant countries concentrate on labour-intensive manufacturing (such as clothing, leather goods and handicrafts).

These predictions are partially, but not fully, borne out by the evidence. Among rich countries, there is a clear demarcation between the relatively empty countries (the US, Canada, Australia, etc.) which are the world's major primary producers and exporters and densely populated

Europe which exports only manufactures and services, and imports primary products. Among poor countries, there is a similar division between thinly populated resource-rich Africa and, to a lesser extent, Latin America and densely populated east and south Asia. Looking at the world as a whole, it is also true that east and south Asia are the major producers and exporters of labour-intensive manufactures and services, the west and Japan produce mainly capital-intensive manufactures and services (with the sparsely populated countries among them also exporting primary products on a large scale), while Africa and Latin America (with a few exceptions) concentrate on primaries.

However, this has not always been the case. Till the 1960s, populous Asia was not a significant exporter of manufactures (except for the most labour-intensive variety of the most labour-intensive manufacture, cotton textiles). Its participation in world trade was marginal, limited to primaries like tea, jute, rubber, tin, etc., and its role in the international trading system not too different from those of Africa and Latin America. The 1960s changed all this.

EMPIRICAL EVIDENCE ON FPE

Possibly more important in its implications than the Heckscher–Ohlin theory is the FPE theorem in the variation that we have developed. What it claims is that free trade either equalizes factor prices or leaves capital-scarce countries with a higher return to capital than capital-rich countries. It follows that if capital mobility were to supplement free trade, there would be a mass exodus of capital from the rich countries to the poor ones till capital–labour ratios in both converged on the same diversification zone (though not on the same value within it) and factor prices would indeed be equalized. This has major implications for international income inequalities. It suggests that these would be sharply reduced by free trade plus capital mobility. They would not vanish altogether since per capita incomes depend not only on wages and returns to capital (which would be equalized) but also on the quantities of capital per head (which would not, though they would be brought within the same diversification zone).

However, until the 1960s, there was little evidence either of a higher rate of return to capital in the poor labour-abundant countries or of a headlong flight of capital from the rich world to them. International capital flows, by and large, were confined to movements within the advanced world. Vast differences in wages and per capita incomes persisted and showed little sign of narrowing.

Why were the predictions of the FPE model so totally falsified by reality before 1960? The logic of the model is ironclad, so the problem lies in its assumptions. We focus specifically on two: CRS and perfect mobility of goods.

Before the decade of the 1960s, the Smithian factor of economies of scale was at least as important a determinant of trade as Ricardian comparative advantage. Since Heckscher–Ohlin theory was based on the assumptions of CRS and of perfect mobility of goods, it could not take into account the consequences of economies of scale in a world market that was segmented by transport costs and other trade barriers into regional sub-markets of varying size. Scale economies were absolutely pervasive in manufacturing, so manufacturers located in large markets (as against those based in small local markets) could achieve these economies without incurring the high cost of penetrating a foreign market.

Densely populated poor countries lacked such large internal markets for manufactures on account of at least three distinct reasons:

1. Low national income imposed an outer limit to their demand for any good.
2. Low per capita income meant, because of Engel's Law, that even the fraction of national income spent on manufactures was small.
3. A high density of population relative to land and capital meant that the returns to labour, the one universally owned resource, were low relative to the returns to property. This resulted in an income distribution polarized between a microscopic elite and a mass of the very poor with no significant middle class. Such an income distribution precluded the rise of a large market for any single manufacture. The very poor could not afford any manufactures beyond the most elementary necessities. The very rich were too few to buy any single good in large quantity; they spent their incomes instead on a large variety of products, all in amounts insufficient to support a mass market.

In consequence, manufacturers based in poor countries, despite their lower wage costs, could not effectively compete with rich-country producers. This is because in most industries, the scale consideration outweighed relative factor costs in determining profitability. There were exceptions, of course: highly labour-intensive industries (such as cotton textiles), industries not amenable to standardization and mass production (such as handicrafts) and industries with negligible transport cost. But for the overwhelming bulk of manufactures, the potential comparative advantage of poor, low-wage economies was nullified by diseconomies of small scale.

In primary production, on the other hand, countries with high land/labour ratios had a comparative advantage, not only because of cheap arable land for agriculture but also because the larger the surface area, the higher the probability of specific geographic advantages such as mineral content or specific types of climate or topography. The densely populated poor countries could not compete with richer rivals in manufacturing, or with the thinly populated countries in primary production. They, therefore, remained peripheral players in the world economy.

From the 1960s, however, changes in technology, nature of the market, distribution of worldwide wealth and the world trading regime reduced the importance of transport costs and economies of scale in world trade:

1. A long-term process of gradual dismantling of trade barriers began with the Kennedy Round in the 1960s and culminated eventually in the establishment of the WTO.
2. Technological changes included containerization and deep-draught freighters that reduced shipping costs, the IT revolution that minimized communication and information costs, and 'just-in-time' management technology which eliminated warehousing and storage. The increased uncertainty of a globalized business environment prompted other changes in technology— businesses tended to discard fixed equipment (which

created long runs of cheaply mass-produced goods but committed firms rigidly to particular products and processes) in favour of flexible specialization based on electronically controlled multipurpose tools that could be adapted at a moment's notice to entirely different methods and products.

3. As incomes rose worldwide, demand became increasingly sophisticated. Quality, exclusiveness and variety became major concerns for the consumer, rather than mere cheapness (which is what large-scale technology could deliver). There was an increased preference for high-value goods whose material content (and therefore transport cost) was low relative to their prices.

4. Finally, the geography of world affluence changed: the world's wealth was redistributed from a primarily North Atlantic locus to the Middle East (because of the oil price explosion of the 1970s) and the Pacific (because of the rapid growth, first of Japan and California in the 1950s and 1960s, and then of the Asian Tigers). This dispersion of global wealth made the rich markets of the world accessible to the poorer countries at lower transport costs.

As the importance of transport costs and scale economies dwindled, the conditions necessary for FPE were gradually approximated, and the theorem was increasingly fulfilled. Labour-intensive manufacturing migrated to East and South Asia, creating the Asian Miracle, while the capital-abundant West and Japan concentrated on increasingly capital-intensive industries, ultimately specializing in those with a very high human- and physical-capital content— the research-intensive knowledge industries. Wages rose all over Asia, but more rapidly in countries with small populations than in those with large labour surpluses. In the West, the return to capital rose while the demand for, and return to, labour stagnated, giving rise to long-term economic recession and unemployment despite high profits. The prosperity enjoyed by Asia was not shared by Africa or Latin America because the comparative advantage of the latter lay not in labour-intensive, but in natural resource-intensive production. Much of the economic history of the last fifty years is explained by this process.

The Rybczynski theorem describes the consequences of factor (say, capital) accumulation on the production structure of an economy under free trade. Those countries where capital grew rapidly (e.g. the pioneers in the Asian Miracle) gradually lost their comparative advantage in labour-intensive production to others that had lagged behind and switched to relatively less labour-intensive activities. This explains the sequence in which industrialization spread in Asia: the original Gang of Four (Korea, Taiwan, Hong Kong, Singapore) lost their most labour-intensive industries to the newly industrializing countries (NICs) (Thailand, Malaysia, Indonesia), and these in turn were followed by Vietnam and, eventually, by China and India.

The Stolper–Samuelson theorem focuses on the impact of trade liberalization and restriction on income distribution. It highlights the sharp contradiction between the interests of labour in labour-abundant and capital-abundant countries—while labour in the West would gain from trade restriction, Indian labour would lose heavily.

THE OPTIMALITY OF FREE TRADE

Up to this point, our concerns in this chapter have related only to the positive theory of trade—the question of what actually happens as a consequence of free trade. Here we address the normative question of how efficient these consequences are from the viewpoint of society.

Under perfect competition and free trade, profit-maximizing producers opt for the production pattern that yields the largest possible difference between the value of their output at world prices and that of their inputs. If we also assume away externalities so that private costs and returns reflect social costs and returns, producers are evidently maximizing net social value added at world prices. Since the economy has no access to any opportunities for production and internal exchange other than those already being exploited by private producers and no opportunities for external exchange except at the same world prices as those open to private individuals, one can simply do no better. National income at world prices is being maximized.

This does not mean a Pareto improvement for society. There will certainly be some losers from free trade. However, since national income at world prices is being maximized, the gains of the gainers must exceed the losses of the losers, so that *if lump-sum transfers are possible*, losers can be compensated without the gainers sacrificing all their gains.

There are of course a number of riders to this proposition. First, if there are economies of scale, competitive equilibrium may be disrupted and the maximization result may not hold. Second, external economies and diseconomies are not rare aberrations but pretty much universal phenomena in modern economies. Finally, lump-sum transfers—sudden, unannounced, unexpected redistributions—simply cannot occur, at least in democratic societies. If redistribution assumes the form of taxes and subsidies, it will be expected and will then impair the incentives to work, save, invest and take risks, thus possibly neutralizing the positive effects of free trade on national income.

Despite this nihilism about the theoretical arguments for free trade, there is a near-universal consensus among mainstream economists on its benefits. This is based only in part on comparative advantage. Major factors in the case for free trade are Smithian economies of scale due to the widening of markets, the stimulus to efficiency due to intensified competition, access to cutting-edge technology and wider choice of products and inputs. Equally important are the disastrous consequences of most trade restrictions first spelled out in Adam Smith's famous attack on mercantilism.

Let us examine the standard arguments for trade restrictions. We begin with the more familiar but less literate arguments:

1. An argument, once commonly heard but now less so, is the mercantilist one that import restrictions improve the balance of payments. What this ignores are the unintended consequences. If we succeed in reducing imports, the demand that these imports used to fulfil is left unsatisfied. It is deflected on to other goods that are potentially exportable, thus inducing a matching contraction in exports. Only if aggregate demand is reduced would the trade balance improve—but then, import restriction would be unnecessary.

2. A pseudo-nationalistic argument is that import restrictions protect domestic producers against foreign competitors. What they actually do is to raise domestic prices above world prices. So, unless they depress world prices more than they widen the margin between them

and the domestic price, they in fact injure the domestic consumer. A country that is too insignificant in the world market to affect the world price cannot affect foreign producers at all; it can only protect domestic producers against domestic consumers.

3. A more sophisticated version of this argument is the *optimal tariff* theory. This concedes the point made in the last paragraph but assumes that the country has some monopoly power in trade. By curtailing its imports, it can reduce their world price; by restricting its exports, it can drive up their world price. By limiting its participation in world trade, it can manipulate its terms of trade to its best advantage. The assumption, of course, is that its trading partners will not retaliate. This is possible if they are all too small. But if some are individually large enough also to affect world prices, the initial trade restriction may set off a spiral of retaliation and counter-retaliation that ends only with the total destruction of trade itself.

4. The oldest and most widely accepted argument for trade restriction is the *infant industry* argument. This assumes that industries acquire efficiency through experience. A new industry, if protected through this learning process, will eventually compete effectively in the world market. Of course, if the economies of experience are all internal, if their costs are all borne by, and their benefits all accrue to, one firm, this would not constitute a case for protection. If the discounted value of the eventual benefits exceeded the initial costs, the firm can finance the initial losses itself and protection will be unnecessary. If the eventual benefits fall short of the initial costs, protection will not be worthwhile. Thus, a plausible case for protection

requires that the learning process should generate external economies. For example, a firm in a new industry may have to invest in labour training, creating a skilled labour force which may leave it before it has even recovered its investment. This could justify temporary protection, but an optimal policy would be to subsidize only the labour training process. A more serious problem with infant industry tariffs may be the refusal of the infant to grow up. Once an industry is established with protection, vested interests develop around it and it becomes politically impregnable—protection can no longer be withdrawn. What is more, the industry anticipates this and therefore does not undertake the costly investment in learning on which the plea for protection was based. Infant protection gradually shades into geriatric care.

Most of the arguments for trade restriction are fallacious. Those restrictions that have some, though limited, value generally target distortions in sectors of the economy other than trade (like skill formation or capital market imperfection) and should ideally be replaced by measures aimed directly at the source of distortion itself (such as a subsidy based on employment in an industry that trains skilled labour). The general consensus among mainstream economists in support of free trade does have a solid basis in economic logic.

SUMMARY

The major causes of international trade are the economies of scale that accompany the growth of the market and the gains from the realization of comparative advantage when people can specialize in what they can do best. Heckscher and Ohlin hypothesized that the main basis of comparative advantage among trading countries lay in differences in factor endowment. The Heckscher–Ohlin model had major implications: (1) that free trade, supplemented where necessary by free capital mobility, would equalize factor prices worldwide even when labour is internationally immobile (FPE); (2) that the growth of any factor in any country would, at constant commodity prices, increase the output intensive in the increasing input and reduce the other output (the Rybczynski theorem); and (3) that protection of any good would shift income distribution in favour of the factor used intensively by the protected industry (the Stolper–Samuelson theorem).

Empirical evidence, while possibly neutral about the factor endowments hypothesis, was however definitely contrary to FPE before 1960. The crucial problems seemed to be with the assumptions of CRS and zero transport cost. The unrealistic nature of these assumptions prior to 1960 resulted in conclusions which were at wide variance with reality—there was no indication during this period either of an exodus of capital from the capital-rich to the labour-abundant economies or of a convergence in wages and per capita incomes. From the decade of the 1960s, however, there were major changes in technology, in the composition of world demand and the geography of global affluence that sharply reduced the importance of transport cost and economies of scale so that FPE could come into its own. Dramatic changes occurred in the patterns of production and trade along with a massive influx of capital from the capital-rich world to labour-abundant Asia, and rapid convergence in wages and per capita incomes. The role of international trade as the major channel for the transmission of economic growth came to the fore as it had been in the late nineteenth century.

Apart from the causes and consequences of free trade, there was also the question of its social desirability. In the absence of externalities, perfect competition and free trade, along with appropriate lump-sum transfers, would ensure that everyone is at least as well-off as under any alternative allocation (and some are better off). However, the pervasiveness of externalities and the unrealism of the perfect competition and lump-sum transferability assumptions undermine the value of this proposition.

Though the theoretical case for free trade has only limited applicability, the arguments for trade restriction are even more fatally flawed. It is improbable that they will ever dent the consensus among economists in favour of free trade—a consensus based not only on considerations of comparative advantage, but also those of economies of scale, intensified competition, freer flows of technology and extended choice of products and inputs.

PROBLEM

1. In 1793, King George III of England sent his ambassador George Macartney to Qian Lung, the emperor of China, with gifts and a proposal for an expansion of trade. In response, the emperor, while commending the king for his spirit of respectful submission in paying tribute, said that China was far superior to the barbarians across the seas in every possible field that she had nothing to gain from trading with them. Assuming, as some ardent Sinophiles do, that the emperor was right on his facts, what do you think of his logic?

Epilogue

We are at the end of our present journey. In the course of it, we have neglected many fascinating byways and skirted many areas of our discipline that we would certainly have explored, had our compass been wider and our travels longer. As it is, even the very brief excursion into economic theory will have provoked the reader to ask a wide range of questions that most certainly deserve answers. Here are a few such questions:

1. We have catalogued the many benefits of free trade. Why then have governments, the world over and throughout history, used protection as their instrument of preference in their foreign economic transactions? Why, for example, did India, for more than forty years after independence, cling to a system of comprehensive control of trade that involved an average tariff rate of 170 per cent and innumerable non-tariff barriers?

2. The Stolper–Samuelson theorem shows that in labour-abundant countries, free trade raises the returns to labour while protection benefits capital. Why then do labour unions and Leftist parties and organizations,

237

who claim to represent the interests of labour in these countries, unanimously excoriate free trade and strongly advocate near-autarchic policies?

3. What light, if any, does our theorizing shed on the relative economic status of different countries? Why was the world of the sixteenth and seventeenth centuries dominated by continental Asia, by the Ming and Manchu empires in China, the Mughals in India and the Ottomans in west Asia, and what accounts for the dramatic reversal of fortune thereafter that made industrial Europe and North America the dominant powers in the world economy? Is the development race slowly shifting back in favour of Asia over the last few decades, and, if so, why?

4. The scientific and technological achievements of the western world over the last fifty years have no parallel in human history. And according to received wisdom, rapid scientific and technological progress is the secret of economic development. Yet, the western world, the nerve centre of these scientific miracles, has experienced continued economic stagnation over this period while low-tech Asia has prospered spectacularly. Why?

5. What are the economic consequences of political institutions (of democracy, for instance)? Does democracy foster or retard economic development?

6. One would expect that political democracy, with its equality of voting power, would ensure economic equality as well. Why then is the world full of democracies with high—and often increasing—degrees of economic inequality (such as the US)?

These are all questions that are legitimate and highly relevant to any student of economics. Unfortunately, the answers to these questions—where they do exist—lie within the realm of political economy. Since I have chosen, in this short volume, to restrict myself to the elements of the much narrower field of pure economic theory, they lie, at present, beyond my scope. I hope, however, in the not-too-distant future, to attempt the rather foolhardy task of answering them.

Acknowledgements

I am profoundly indebted to many generations of my students at the School of International Studies, Jawaharlal Nehru University (JNU), New Delhi, whose endless curiosity and interest caused me to question myself and my discipline in ways that led ultimately to this book. Among them, I would like to single out one of my oldest students, Geeta Gouri, for the trouble she took in reading and commenting on the earlier drafts of this book. A much later student, Malabika Pal, shared with me the teaching of the course from which this book originated, and therefore contributed significantly to its development. I must also mention a current student, Sugandha Huria, whose meticulous and painstaking empirical work has helped in confirming some of the ideas expressed in the book.

I am grateful to Rudrangshu Mukhopadhyay and the *Telegraph* for permission to use material from my articles in the newspaper in the chapter on national income. I am also indebted to Shabnam Srivastav and Radhika Marwah for their immense help in getting this book published, to Radhika and Aditi Muraleedharan for their editorial work, and to Debosmita Sarkar for her work in publicizing it.

I owe my deepest debt to my wife, Indrani, and my daughter, Brishti. Without their constant encouragement and continuous support, this book would never have been written. Brishti went through the earlier drafts of the book, rectifying my errors, reprimanding me sternly for their frequency, and suggesting lines of thought for me to develop. My debt to her is beyond measure or expression.